Fifty Shapes of G

John W. Matthews

Published by Zoey – epublishinghelp.com
ISBN: 978-2-1886-2155-0

For my wife Patty, our five children and their spouses, and our
eleven grandchildren . . . who all embody unique, beautiful
'shapes of grace'

Table of Contents

Preface

As I approach my seventy-fifth birthday, having been retired for five years, I find myself reflecting quite a bit on what I have experienced and what I have learned. Although I probably know more now than I have ever known before, I am continually reminded of how little I really know, given the complexity of the world and the expanse of the universe. I went to college and majored in philosophy and religion so that I could know more and - in that way - have a better grasp on life. It was there in my search for certainty and security in the early 1970s that I was exposed to the Reformed theology of Dr. Francis Schaeffer. He was a very conservative Presbyterian pastor who studied under Cornelius Van Til and J. Gresham Machen at the conservative (fundamentalist) Westminster Theological Seminary. Schaeffer, with his wife Edith, went on to form the L'Abri community in Switzerland, designed to welcome all, especially students, to a place of 'shelter' where their theological questions and psychological needs could be honestly – and fully - resolved. Feasting on his books and spending time with Dr. Schaeffer seemed to offer me an invulnerable, intellectual, Christian foundation for life, or so I thought. He believed and passionately taught about 'Propositional Revelation,' that is, the 'true truth, the propositions' that God has revealed in the Bible, and that one can know absolutely and believe in unquestionably. I found in Francis Schaeffer the comprehensive worldview I desired and the truth that the philosophers I was studying in college could only hope for. I carried this over-abundant confidence (arrogance?) off to Luther Seminary in the Fall of 1971, armed with God's absolute, propositional truth that could withstand the Biblical relativity that I heard was being taught at the seminary. At Luther Theological Seminary, I was humbled and subsequently came to learn that my pursuit of knowledge had only begun and would be a life-long journey. There, I began to understand that every life experience had more to teach me about ultimate things, and that the Biblical witness was multivalent and beautifully complex. Francis Schaeffer's over-confidant apologetic version of Christian theology began to recede for me at the same time that a more accurate, authentic, and humble understanding of the Christian faith opened before my eyes. I was discovering that there was SO much more depth and breadth to the Christian experience and tradition than I had come to know in Schaeffer's L'Abi community. I have been on that journey of discovery ever since. In the Church and the university teaching I have done, I often remembered what one seminary professor, Gerhard Frost, shared fifty years ago with our class on Christian Education: "Remember that answers kill, but questions give life." Socrates, long before that, said, "I know only one thing - that I know nothing." His personal confession is now ironically referred to as 'Socratic ignorance' when, in fact, said ignorance is the epitome of wisdom. In my retirement, I want to listen more and talk less; at least, it feels that way. The '50 Shapes of Grace' in front of you reflects some of the wonder and complexity I have experienced, more often in listening and questioning than talking and answering. I have discovered God - and God's grace - in places I never dreamt would hold it. I have learned that the revelation of God in Jesus Christ is not exclusive but rather one place among many to experience the wonder of creation and the grace of God.

Introduction

Most of life's experiences - certainly relationships - include elements of grace. Grace can be defined as 'gift, kindness, favor, courtesy, enrichment, forgiveness, divine assistance, salvation,' etc. Perhaps that has a ring of something religious from God that ought to reside in all of life's relationships. And, while the Church may claim to be the primary custodian and guardian of divine grace as understood as the action of God in the life, death, and resurrection of Jesus, and like Judaism, stakes claim to the action of God in the sacred history of Israel and Torah, and like Islam may hold the title to God's final revelation in the Quran, such claims ought to compliment, never limit or monopolize, the breadth and depth of God's gracious blessing on all creation, a grace that leaves virtually no space and place untouched. Relationships - like people - are *simil justis et peccator* (simultaneously blessed and broken), hence always in need of grace. Relationships - like people - exhibit elements, degrees, even different 'shapes of grace.' To not recognize these elements, degrees, and shapes of grace is to miss out on SO much of life's richness, as intended by the author of life, the redeemer of humankind. To allow life's dark shadows to eclipse such significant moments of grace is really an insult to the creator who faithfully blesses and continues to sustain all of life, with grace. The people and programs here described have enriched my life in inestimable ways; through them, grace has been experienced in powerful, even if - at times - broken ways. A beautiful example of this marvelous complimentary relationship between God's more ultimate revelations of grace in Jesus, Israel/Torah, Quran etc., and our experience of grace in the ordinary is the well-known 18th century Danish hymn by Nikolaij Frederik Severin Grundtvig, *O Day Full of Grace* (Den signede dag som vi nu ser). Made familiar to many by the F. Melius Christiansen anthem of the same name, I first heard this composition sung by the Concordia Choir, directed by Christiansen's son, Paul, when I enrolled at Concordia College in Moorhead in 1968. The poetic words of the hymn speak of that complementarity:

O day, full of grace, which we behold, now gently to view ascending; thou over the earth thy reign un-fold, good cheer to all mortals lending, that children of light in every clime may prove that the night is ending.

How blest was that gracious midnight hour, when God in our flesh was given; then flushed the dawn with light and power, that spread o'er the darkened heaven; then rose o'er the world that Sun divine, which gloom from our hearts hath driven.

Yea, were every tree endowed with speech, and every leaflet singing; they never with praise His worth could reach, though earth with their praise were ringing, who fully could praise the Light of Life, who light to our souls is bringing.

As birds in the morning sing God's praise, His fatherly love we cherish for giving to us this day of grace, for life that shall never perish. His Church He hath kept these thousand years and hungering souls did nourish.

Now softly, the light of Pentecost is shining its beams around us. God's blessings for us cannot be lost, as brooks in the fields surround us. And leave in their wake the woods and fields, the bright summer green. astounds us.

John W. Matthews

With joy we depart for our fatherland, where God our Father is dwelling; where ready for us His mansions stand, where Heaven with praise is swelling. And there we shall walk in endless light, with blest ones His praise forth telling.

My hope is that the following sacred examples of 50 Shapes of Grace will stimulate you - the reader - to perceive the marvelous shapes of grace in the ordinary experiences of your life. Eyes, ears, and hearts that choose to be open and vulnerable can experience divine grace in most every person and in nearly every place. It is often an experience of grace that provides the light, the hope, and the energy for people to risk returning and attempt redeeming broken relationships. From the hymn, 'O Day Full of Grace,' we hear: "God's blessings for us cannot be lost, as brooks in the fields surround us and in their wake the woods and fields, the bright summer green astounds us." The examples below show shapes of grace in the 'brooks, woods and fields,' in our families, marketplaces, university classrooms, friendships, and our strengths and weaknesses. I hope you risk opening your 'eyes, ears, and heart.'

1

My Cornerstone of Grace

Because it is the primal, foundational, generative, and example par excellence of grace for anyone calling themselves Christian, I am choosing to begin this collection of 'shapes of grace' with the cornerstone I know in the person of Jesus, the Christ, the incarnate, Emmanuel, God-with-us. While there are SO many places where the Almighty-Creator God has entered creation in graceful ways, it is Jesus, the Jewish son of a carpenter in Galilea twenty centuries ago, who spoke and acted in powerful ways that helped bridge the seemingly impossible chasm for billions of people between Heaven and earth, the divine and the human. Often divine grace is synonymous with this Jesus because of the cardinal role he played, the sacrificial gift he offered for humanity, a gift that keeps on giving into the Twenty-first century. Grace - in Jesus - has been seen by Christians as God's supreme revelation for the world's salvation. The fifty-seven examples and stories which follow are not intended in any way to underestimate the grace of God known in Torah, Jesus, and the Quran (to mention just three), but to broaden our vison, hopefully to perceive the graciousness and goodness of God infiltrating virtually every square inch of creation, as we know it. Let's continue as we read about '50 Shapes of Grace' beyond these three 'big ones.'

2

Grace in Retirement

In August of 2019, I retired from the ELCA ministry after forty-four years of congregational work and (simultaneously) eighteen years of adjunct teaching at Augsburg University in Minneapolis and Rochester. I had also been an emergency police/fire chaplain in every community I lived in and a US Army reserve chaplain for five years in the late 1980s. I thought I was prepared for retirement, having nurtured some hobbies (soap carving, ping pong, reading, traveling, etc.), and I had no anxiety about the retirement I faced. I had no plans for interim ministry with congregations in transition now that I was almost seventy years old. Patty and I could enjoy retired life, having minimal commitments and freedom to choose each day's schedule. Soon into retirement, the world was shut down with the COVID epidemic (March 2020), and we hunkered down to a solitary life at home, only venturing out to get groceries and take drives to nowhere. We, too, watched multiple television series (wasn't Yellowstone wonderful?) and plenty of news shows. About two years into retirement, I would often be asked, "So, how is retirement going for you and Patty?" Fair enough. Most people wonder about such things. As I reflected on how to answer that honest and timely question, I most often responded, "Well, it's really good. But, you know, I feel somewhat disoriented. It's not a bad thing. We are having a good time. It's just different. I'm not sure exactly what to point toward or what lies ahead. Just disoriented." Until this point in life, there was always something predictable ahead: graduate from high school, go to college, get a job, get married, have children, watch them grow-up, see them graduate, change jobs, bury their parents, etc. etc. Now I ask, "I wonder what's next?" I am not sure. I don't know which direction to go, given so many options. The voice of grace then speaks to me, "Just lean into it. Don't fret about goals, accomplishments, and what is next. Take-in today. Enjoy the people and events that come your way. Make some plans if that helps." Retirement is a new chapter. Uncharted waters. Yet, good waters. Grace means trust . . . the process, the future, God.

3

Grace in Simple Questions

An irritating habit of mine (I am told) is to ask people in public places, like a waiter in a restaurant, who they will be voting for in the upcoming election. It is not irritating to me because I like doing that; rather, it is irritating to others who say, "Why in the heck did you ask that?" I usually respond with, "I am not asking it to have an argument; I am just interested to know more about people." Most often, if not always, such people hesitate momentarily but then share their thoughts. I say: "Thank you for sharing, and I think I will have a piece of dessert." I may be somewhat inappropriate for asking such questions; there's not much grace in putting people on the spot, especially during times in our country when there is such polarity among people. The grace I experience is in how genuinely people respond. These waitpersons are taking a risk, not knowing how I will respond, or others at the table. Their taking a risk is what I say is a gift of grace to me, a stranger asking them a rather personal question. Often, it helps to inquire about the meaning of one of their tattoos; again, most people appreciate others taking an interest in their life. I plan to keep doing this; at least, until I get accosted or told to shut-up. My hope is to create a safe space for people to share what they think or feel. I am so glad these kind folks take a gracious risk with me. People are beautiful, aren't they? Especially when they open-up.

Friends

4

Grace in Disagreement

Pat is someone I would call a true friend. Over the past twenty years, we have worked together, laughed, and shared our ups and downs. We have the deepest respect for each other and seek each other out for advice and honest response. I would call Pat a true friend. For a variety of reasons, Pat and I come to different conclusions on the topic of homosexuality; we disagree on whether gay, Lesbian, and bisexual people are the way they are because of design or decision. Both of us have gay friends and know these our friends to be children of God. Yet, is their gender identity or sexual orientation something they chose or something they were born with? Pat and I view the evidence differently. We understand our conversations with our friends differently. Pat firmly believes that his gay friends and acquaintances would be more in line with God's design were they to find their way back to a heterosexual orientation or accept their homoerotic feelings yet live chaste lives of sexual abstinence. I am not sure that Pat and I will ever agree on this topic, nor view our gay friends the same way. I am not sure what it would take for either of us, or both of us, to see things differently. Yet, Pat is a true friend. We both are religious persons who desire to know and follow God's design for our lives. For me, this is an experience of different shapes of grace. Of course, we each think we perceive things the right way. Grace is that experience of God's presence which allows us to not label our view as light and right and the other as dark and wrong . . . at least not where sincere, committed, loving people attempt to live authentically. One of the shapes that grace has taken is the recognition that God's goodness transcends our human notions of right and wrong. 'God's truth is bigger than both of us.' True friendship is based on respect and love, not total agreement or perfect insight.

5

Grace in (discussing) Politics, Sex and Religion

John, Steve, and I meet off-and-on for breakfast at Perkins, County Road 42, and Cedar Avenue in Apple Valley. John and I are retired; Steve flies for Delta/Endeavor for a few more years. After several exchanges with details about our lives and families, we order the breakfast of choice and launch into significant, albeit usually forbidden, conversations: politics, sex, and religion. Our conversations seem well - informed, thoughtful, and entertaining. During these times of political unrest and cultural polarity, we work hard to stay calm and even harder to give our partners in conversation the benefit of the doubt. We always conclude on a friendly note. We always depart, having touched on significant issues. So, where's the grace in all this? When we first gather - and when we depart - there's always shoulder touches, smiles and jokes. (The unspoken thought I think we all have is, "Steve/John/Johnny, next time, will you please get your head out of your axx") We love each other and are very good friends; we disagree about significant subjects and wonder how the other can think the way they do. Grace is the name for sincerely knowing and deeply feeling that 'truth is bigger than all of us.' "Hand me the syrup, please, for my waffle . . . and let's move on to another topic."

6

Grace in the Wisdom of Sages

Almost monthly, a group of retired pastors, theologians, and religious leaders meet to talk about important things. This group involves Jews and Christians, and others who bring 'career-long' questions and convictions to the table. The conversation is rich and meaningful for Tom, Grant, Norman, Cynthia, Ann, Jan, and me. Some topics can resolve; others are of concern and will remain questions. Oh, there's differences, but those usually lead to greater insight and deeper wisdom. I look forward to gatherings like shots in the arm and balm for the soul. Together we've worked on some particular proposals and projects, but most often we just engage in life-giving dialogue. We enjoy the deepest respect for one another and consider this a little taste of eternity. I believe we all think that God is looking down on our get-togethers with a smile. Grace is an appropriate descriptor of those regular meetings. Partly because the normal denominational and interfaith designators don't matter. Just grace.

7

Grace in the Chatter of Friends

Although our small group of friends was already gathering weekly for 'Wednesday Waffles at the Buzz,' it was during the pandemic (2020-21) that our meetings on Zoom, or during the summer months outside, cemented our closeness and created a 'heavenly foretaste of the feast to come.' Yes, we, five old retired guys, and one still working, color our conversations with talk about personal matters, political controversies, medical problems, relational challenges, and church issues. Much like the monthly get-together of the other 'sages' in my life, this weekly gathering is something I really look forward to and hate to miss. I think the make-up of our group and the dynamics of our conversations reveal a deep sense of trust and provide a zone of real safety. These two-trust and safety - are things that I no longer take for granted; in our world that has become severely polarized, such places of honest conversation and fun times can be hard to find. We meet for approximately an hour, order coffee and fantastic waffles of every kind, and experience stories (true or not), validation of our struggles, challenge for our narrow-mindedness and learning of new things . . . every time. Lee is, by self-designation, our Wednesday Waffle Coordinator (WWC), Brad is our resident (retired) physician, Mark our (retired) electrical engineer, Scott our (retired) contractor, Robert our still employed voice of reality, and me, retired from parish ministry but primarily in charge of never letting things get too pious or too serious.

In addition to this weekly gathering and our weekly chaplains' meetings, I have also become involved in ENGAGE (Lutherans for Gun Violence Prevention). This weekly hour-and-a-half Zoom call involves about seven people who are all passionate about making a difference in our violent world. I am a gun owner who is laboring hard for broader gun registration and background checks, safer gun storage laws, and more restrictions on unnecessary semi-automatic weapons on the streets. With my wife, Patty, we are trying to make a difference for our world, especially our dear grandchildren.

8

Grace in Taking Risks

My good friend, David Nimmer, is a journalist who used to write for the Minneapolis Star and later report for WCCO television. In retirement, he loves visiting some Catholic sisters' homes near the north side of Minneapolis. He tells about the 'presence' of these nuns living in the 'hood's heart.' Not only do the nuns befriend and pray for gang members and neighbors often in trouble with the law, but the gang members and neighbors look-out for the nuns. The house is a safe haven for many. David continues to be amazed, as I am when he shares stories from his visits there about the peace and trust often experienced in a part of town that is actually rather unsafe. These Nuns of the Presentation have absorbed so much grace, that fear and distrust have taken leave. A murder not so long ago took place in their front yard. They are still there. . . and will be as long as God gives them life and grace. I stand in awe every time David returns and shares more episodes of life and death in the hood. Couldn't happen without grace.

9

Grace in 'Little Free Libraries'

In 2008, I was having breakfast with a member of the Afton congregation I served, Memorial Lutheran Church. Todd Bol, a member of Memorial, and I regularly shared a meal together; he loved pork sausage hash and Jelly toast with a couple of easy-over eggs. I most often stuck to my usual potato pancakes, bacon, and apple sauce. Todd was a 'creative' to the max, having worked at 3M, but was now a private entrepreneur dreaming about ways to make the world a better place. Todd's entire family belonged to Memorial Lutheran Church, and/but Todd was very transparent about his questions and doubts (I love that about my friends), and he thought of himself as more agnostic. As we sat that morning at Key's Café in Hudson, after he ordered his hash, he said he was wrapping-up and selling his last creation, a nursing exchange program with the Philippines. Todd said, "Here is my new idea, Pastor John." I thought to myself, "Here we go again, Todd, but will this new idea put bread on your table?" Todd's wife, Susan, was extremely patient and a very loving wife who taught school. She was somehow able to maintain her sanity while Todd tried to change the world . . . with little compensation for his ideas. Todd went on that morning (sketching on a white paper napkin stained with maple syrup), saying, "The world needs people reading more. I want to create a movement that helps families, especially children, read more at no cost." Now he's sketching a picture of what looked like a little house with a front door that opens. He continued, "We could have these little houses all over neighborhoods, and people could 'take a book; share a book.' No cost, just folks exchanging books, and having neighborly conversations. It will also create community." I thought, "What a great idea . . . but then most of Todd's ideas that I thought were fantastic never quite took flight." I wondered how he would finance this and who would run it. Todd shared that he had a friend in Madison, Wisconsin, who he thought would be interested in investing-in and co-leading the effort. Forward fifteen years, the Little Free Library movement has registered 150,000 placements in fifty states, 120 countries and seven continents. Virtually every city I visit has one or more LFLs blessing their community. Todd had trouble with the organized church, observing what many of us do: fraud, hypocrisy, sex scandals, country club mentalities and the like. Riding shotgun to Todd's reverent agnosticism was a deep love and commitment to the simple love of Jesus, with people living for others. Every time I pass a Little Free Library I am reminded of the origin of that grace-filled movement: a syrup-stained napkin at Key's Café in Hudson, Wisconsin. Todd died in the Fall of 2018 of pancreatic cancer. I was honored to be asked to officiate at his funeral service. His wife, Sue and his children, Allison and Austin - with their family and friends - gathered at Bradshaw Funeral Home in Stillwater, Minnesota, for a memorial service to celebrate the life of an agnostic person who displayed the grace of God in very creative ways. Can grace and agnosticism live together?

10

Grace in an Ordinary Sermon

Dave Beck is one of my dearest friends. Our relationship of about 30 years has involved near weekly conversations about. . . most everything. My memory takes me back about 25 years to a Monday morning conversation with Dave about Sunday's sermon; he is one parishioner who seriously engaged with every message I preached. Although I can't recall the assigned text or the topic for that particular day, Dave reminds me that I abruptly changed directions, set aside the given text, and preached about Jesus in the boat with his disciples. Jesus appealed to their selfish desire for more fish, and they took him at his word. This sermon was particularly relevant for Dave, he told me later, because he was bothered by the amount of food that CONAGRA (where he worked) threw away each month. He wondered if that excess food could be routed to needy people. Dave ended-up working food procurement for Meals on Wheels. These twenty-five years later, millions of people across America have been fed because of the left-over food by major corporations. It came together after that sermon: Jesus multiplied loaves of bread through sharing; Jesus provided more fish by creative angling; Jesus (through Dave Beck) used left-over food to feed hungry people here in America. I was humbled to learn that 'an average sermon' might stimulate such a creative use of resources. Sounds like grace to me.

11

Grace in An Atheist's 'Unbelief'

I got to know Fred while serving on a board that oversaw the work of World Without Genocide, directed by Ellen Kennedy and located at the Wm. Mitchell-Hamline School of Law in St. Paul. I was a Lutheran pastor, and Fred was a Holocaust survivor. We became very good friends and shared many meals together. Thank you, Sandra for sharing Fred with me for all those lunches away. My assumption (which sometimes gets us in trouble) was that because Fred - and some of his family - had survived the Holocaust, they would (still) be observant Jews. I knew all about Orthodox, Reform, Conservative, and Reconstructionist Jews, but until Fred, I had not met an atheist Jew. I had only known the term 'secular Jew' when referring to those Jews who lived somewhat outside one of the four traditions. As we know, being a Jew can mean practicing Judaism, but it can also mean (simply) being born of a Jewish mother. Now, I suppose a Lutheran and an atheistic Jew could both perceive their conversation to be one of implicit, if not explicit, proselytization; that is, each might come to the conversation with hopes that at the end of the day, or even many conversations, the other would come to believe as they did. But, as our relationship unfolded, not only didn't the proselytization occur, but a genuine curiosity continued to fuel our conversations. Fred continued to wonder what made me (a Christian) believe certain things; I continued to wonder what made him, an (atheist) Jew believe certain things. And that curiosity continued, but increasingly with deeper respect and 'holy envy.' Both Fred and I gathered to experience the humanity and wisdom of someone quite different in bloodline, experience and commitments. It was never, "You are wrong, and I am right!" More often, it was, "Wow, I never thought of that before!" In Fred, I came to experience the grace (dare I say 'Grace of God?') which lies at life's center. His sense of wonder accompanied Fred's humility, humor, wisdom, and sensitivity, embrace of me as an 'other,' and his knowing that our friendship is a taste of eternity, even though neither of us knows what shape that will finally take. I am so glad I no longer limit the grace of God to Jesus, Jesus, only Jesus. God is so much bigger, and I have been blessed to learn more about God and grace, even from an atheist Jew.

12

Grace in an Honest 'No!'

Henry Oertelt is a Jewish survivor of five concentration camps, including Auschwitz, his last 'stop,' near the end of the Second World War. Henry was aged 12-24 during the Nazi times in Germany. His experiences are recorded in 'An Unbroken Chain - My Journey through the Nazi Holocaust,' a book he published in 2000. I first met Henry in a dialogue one Sunday morning in 1988 with John Gallos on WCCO television. After that serendipitous meeting, a friendship began with Henry – and his wife, Inge – that brought him to every congregation I served: Prince of Peace Lutheran Church in Brooklyn Park, Trinity Lutheran in Moorhead, Memorial Lutheran Church in Afton, and Grace Lutheran Church in Apple Valley. Each year, around the commemoration of Yom Ha Shoah (Holocaust Remembrance), I would invite survivors or Rabbis to speak at the congregation during worship. Over twenty-three years Henry came multiple times to tell his story of the 'unbroken chain.' On one of those occasions, at Memorial in Afton, on one of those occasions, when during our dialogue sermon that I asked a 'Christian' question during our dialogue sermon, "Henry, was there any time when you were in Auschwitz that you experienced the presence of God?" He curtly said, "No!" Then ensued an uncomfortable silence. As you might imagine, I – the pastor and moderator – was stunned and speechless. What could I say next to move the sermon along? This show-stopper of a response seemed embarrassing; somehow, it felt authentic and real. I did find a way to continue, but I can't remember what I said. I cautiously and humbly kept things moving. I have never forgotten that moment (as you can tell), and it ushered in a new chapter in my journey to somehow comprehend the depth and despair of that time in history. Grace – meaning truth – does not always come packaged with fancy ribbons and pleasant fragrancies. Henry did not deliver us an answer that made something positive out of a horrendous time. Grace doesn't just mean 'being nice.' However, it can be grace if it opens our eyes to what is really important. Thanks, Henry, for your truth-telling, your honesty, your grace. I have memorized your tattooed number from Auschwitz: B-11291. May you rest in peace.

Family and (sometimes dys-) Function

13

Grace in Doing Ones Best

When I look back over my childhood and up-bringing, I have much for which to be thankful. Compared to so many people I meet, I feel extremely grateful for having had a very loving father and an unbelievably kind mother. Sadly though, they both died at a relatively young age. I would describe my father as a somewhat Stoic, quiet man with diverse interests and a strong sense of morality and responsibility. My Dad was a chemist, by profession at Continental Motors Corporation in Muskegon, Michigan, who loved to hunt and fish, and devoted many years to the Scouting program, of which I was a fortunate recipient. He was a solid role model and one I respected greatly. However, I was told early on that my Dad had quite a temper, was the one who growing-up, would finish the fights his brothers would get into, and who didn't share his feelings very openly. For that reason, although I learned many good things from my Dad, I never learned how to engage others in conflict in what I would call the 'intermediate range.' My Dad could like someone a lot, and he could also write someone off. But the in-between, the intermediate range, where people disagree yet stay connected, my Dad was not that good. Hence, I did not learn how to do that either. I saw in my Dad's life of fifty-nine years so many good qualities; I also saw his deficiencies. I inherited some of those good qualities; I missed having those other things which might have helped me in my later relationships. My Mom was the source of my knowing what unconditional love was about. Never uttering a discouraging word, my Mom always tried to make the best of things and always encouraged my sister and me. I probably was scolded and spanked in my earliest years, for others have said I was a little sh** , but I have no recollection of that. In hindsight, I think that my Mom probably had what today we would call boundary issues; that is, she had difficulty saying 'no' and more difficulty confronting others when she felt violated. I later understood God's unconditional grace precisely because I had seen something similar acted out in my Mom's words and deeds. For that I will be eternally grateful. I do know people who had the opposite experience, where parents were hypercritical and very conditional in their love and acceptance. For those people accepting God's grace is difficult because they never knew it while growing-up. While I have benefited so much from a Mom who lived unconditional grace, I missed growing-up with good boundaries, and so I was often challenged when needing to establish boundaries later in life. From my Dad and Mom, I learned so much, and while some important pieces for life's journey may have been left out, identifying those parts I later found missing has never diminished the gratitude I feel for the grace I came to know. One of the shapes that grace has taken – and I believe will take in eternity - is the love, kindness, and brokenness of parents, doing their very best with what they had. Your parents?

14

Grace Needed in Raising Children

When deciding to have children in our mid-20s, now forty-eight years ago, I can't even remember all the hope and fears that filled my imagination. Of course, we were not going to make all the mistakes others made; we possessed the strength and sensitivity to properly guide and correct their good and bad behavior. Conceive we did, and giving birth took place. For all those years Charlotte (my first wife) and I tried our best to parent our two precious little charges, Sari and Maren. Now, when our children are in their upper 40s, having kids of their own, my feelings fluctuate between deep gratitude and joy at just how such wonderful children could bless our lives and contribute so much to the world in which we live and periodic guilt and regret when I remember the ways I/we could've done better. As a pastor, I was gone way too much; Charlotte, maybe - even from Heaven - wonders if using a wooden spoon on Sari's behind when she misbehaved was the best approach. I'm not looking for easy compliments in sharing this sadness; no matter what anyone says, there are things that simply offset the joy with some regret. Yes, most parents have such feelings; no, they never go away. Truth be told, the gratitude and joy far outweigh the guilt and regret. By God's grace and our dear children's graciousness, I can smile way more than frown laugh way more than cry. I smile, at times, when contemplating this experience of blessing and regret regarding the rearing of children when I think that someday when our kids' kids are grown, they too will celebrate the joy and manage the guilt they feel with their own children. Life is interesting, huh? Grace can be a soothing balm for sometimes heavy hearts.

15

Grace within Dysfunction

Following my sister's death in 2021, I often reflect on the blessings and brokenness I saw in her life of 75 years. Her death resulted from a combination of illnesses; I think she had had a brain tumor, congestive heart failure, diabetes, cancer, blocked arteries, and more. While her last few years involved significant pain in her legs and abdomen, my phone conversations (spanning six hundred miles between our homes) usually included talk of her loneliness and frustration with failed relationships. In the course of her (single) life, she was extremely irresponsible with finances and 'borrowed' money from most of our family and friends. She never quite figured out why these people never came to see her or invited her for a meal. Truth be told, most of them had been used because the 'borrowed' money was never paid back. Hence, their distancing from her was very understandable. My memories of Ann from childhood were quite positive. She was gentle, kind, and concerned about others. Her dreams of being married were persistent, yet never materialized, and she struggled to accept the fact that she would never have a partner to share life's ups and downs. For that, I, too, was extremely sad, but realized that with her relational challenges and financial irresponsibility, she would likely have serious challenges if ever she did marry. Ann's brokenness caused me sadness and a small degree of guilt, never being able to do enough to make her happy. I often thought that true happiness for her would have to come in the next life because it never happened in this one. So where is there grace in the midst of such dysfunction? Surprisingly, I could never figure out, given her large number of physical and relational challenges, how she mustered-up the energy to even get up every morning. I could never understand how she continued to desire living and hoping for things that seemed so far beyond her reach. I often thought, "Wow, God has really implanted persistence and drive in Ann, beyond what I have ever known." Ann's passion and resilience to continue wanting life astounded me! With all her challenges, my sister kept going. Grace within dysfunction. Yes, there it was, in her passionate persistence to keep-on-going, when every step seemed uphill. I sincerely hope Ann has found, in her death, the 'fun' outside of dysfunction. She sure struggled here to find it.

16

Grace in Questionable Humor

I grew-up in a family where explicit and subtle humor was a common part of almost every conversation. I knew my aunts and uncles colored everything with humor and sarcasm, and I soon learned that the same questionable humor was passed-on to my cousins, especially Don, Chuck, and Mary. I learned long-ago that humor is always built on irony, and that funny things are usually expressed at someone's expense. Like the jokester who is falling or the embarrassed person who is seen half naked, laughter occurs most often when someone is compromised or has done something self-effacing. In this way, whenever I think of my uncles or cousins, I always remember they had a joke to offer. Now, one could be taught to be more sensitive and caring, to never make fun of someone else's foible or frailty. However, I was not raised with that sensitivity. I grew-up on jokes about Norwegians, Swedes, Italians, atheists, pietists, Christians, Jews, Whites, Blacks, Hispanics, and healthy and handicapped people. Unfortunately, such making fun of others can too easily express or imply demeaning and derogatory thoughts. In that same growing-up, I was taught to be sensitive-to and caring-of other people in all places and states of life. My home exhibited a profound sensitivity and appreciation for 'otherness' and an appreciation of humor that made fun of all kinds of people. Through the years and in a variety of settings, I was, at times, judged because of my questionable humor. I have tried very hard to remain sensitive and caring of people; I think I understand people's pain and identities. Yet, the grace I find within questionable humor serves to help me manage life's pains and appreciate life's ironies. I no longer apologize. Questionable humor is my lingua franca; in those unlikely and often inappropriate places, I have experienced grace. Therefore, inappropriate is sometimes - for me - very appropriate. I am a Christian, but not a pietist. "Did you hear the one about. . . "

17

Grace and Profanity

One side of my family - the Matthews' side - had incredibly funny people in it, with diverse and colorful personalities. From my grandpa, his boys learned to call everything from their disobedient dog to people they just didn't like "God-damned sons a bitches." And with this 'colorful' language came stories and jokes that curled milk and made even a sailor blush. One uncle in particular - Fred by name - had at the age of 18 enlisted in the US Army Air Corps, serving in WWII for the final years of that conflict as a tail gunner on a B-17 bomber. He was shot down several times, once receiving 'friendly' fire from those on the ground who didn't know he was an American. Fred lived the rest of his life with some degree of PTSD and shell-shock. Fred had a wonderful - yet crude - sense of humor, which I loved, and beneath his rough exterior and macho persona was a heart and a desire to help others. I often told parishioners in Minnesota that, after vacationing in Michigan for a week in the summer, it took me another couple of weeks to drain-off the crude language and dirty stories that I heard and grew-up on and re-enter parish niceness. In my relationships with my uncles and aunts, I learned that beneath the crudeness of some people lies a soul that is struggling to reach-out and love and be loved but whose life experience makes that hard to do. PTSD caused uncle Fred to keep an external guard up that often looked crude and insensitive; yet, I could feel the grace of God in his struggle, and it taught me to look deeper and even enjoy the crude exterior.

Grace can be known in/with/under profanity; Fred's wife, Beverly, and his children - Eileen, Colleen, Rich, and Bryan – can attest to this combination of grace and profanity.

18

Grace in a Blended Family

If grace has been experienced anywhere in my life, it is located in the absolutely blessed relationship I have with my wife, Patty. Words like 'special', ' precious' and 'devoted' can't begin to describe the love and blessing I experience with Patty, my wife of thirty years. She, being divorced, and me, being widowed following the death of my first wife, Charlotte, in 1991, came together in 1995, when I served as Senior Pastor of Trinity Lutheran Church in Moorhead, Minnesota. My daughters, Sari (19) and Maren (16), joined together with Patty's children, Bryan (16), Jodee (14), and Kayla (11), in a blended family of seven, on a journey of discovery that has included the mountain peaks of life and some of the inevitable valleys. Blending two family systems with all the attendant attitudes, traditions, and roles is a huge challenge. There were times Patty and I said to one another, "Maybe we shouldn't have embarked on this journey." We said that not because our love wasn't strong, but because the challenges were pretty intense. Today, these five children (now 48, 46, 46, 44, and 40) are unbelievably supportive of, blessed by, and find enjoyment in their sibling and step-sibling relationships, month by month. Add to that, eleven grandchildren – Addison, Dylan, Tyler, Cole, Jaxon, Quinn, Soren, Paige, Mason, Cora, and Bodie – and we have more than a wonderful quiver full of arrows. Even the word grace fails to capture the blessing of these eleven fully, these five plus spouses, and number one, Patty by name. Grace means love and love means family, one big family in our case. Regarding this blended family journey of peaks and valleys, we began in 1995 . . . I am really glad we took the risk and weathered the storms.

19

Grace as Occasional Presence

I grew up with 28 cousins, most of whom lived in Muskegon during my childhood. I felt very fortunate to be with these cousins a fair amount. In addition to my three (double-related) cousins, Don, Chuck, and Mary, who shared the same four grandparents as me, I spent most of my time with Larry and Eddie. I have such good memories of staying at their houses overnight, and spending many summer afternoons together. After leaving home and moving to Minnesota at age eighteen, our times together were fewer and getting back to Muskegon each summer was really fun. One cousin memory that falls under the 'grace' category was Ed's visits to Minnesota over many years. And even among all of those, it was the time in February 1991, when my first wife, Charlotte, passed away, that I remember Ed coming to visit. I remember he was then on business in Wisconsin and decided to travel five hours to attend her funeral. Because so many cousins lived so far away and the challenge of traveling to snowy Minnesota in winter, having him present those days was especially meaningful. On other occasions, cousins Don, Chuck, Barb, Jean, and Eileen came west for visits. Their presence spelled grace.

20

Grace and the Curse of Cancer

My first wife, Charlotte, was only 34 when the onset of her breast cancer jolted our lives. After a four-year reprieve, it returned, but this time to her brain. Of course, myself and our two daughters - ages twelve and ten - were solidly behind her entering radiation and chemo therapy, hoping and praying that we would be granted more years of life together. The routine was hard but our dream for recovery kept all of us going. Again, a year later, the cancer spread to her lungs, and by the end of 1990, it appeared we would not be winning this battle. Our thoughts and conversations often turned to what life for the 'three of us' would be like after her death. Sadness was the primary emotion, with moments of anger and hours of frustration. I don't think 'acceptance' ever happened before her death in 1991. My religious faith provided strength and perspective, but never joy during this time. So, what about God's grace? Of course, I was blessed with two wonderful daughters that provided reasons-a plenty-to get up each day and keep going. I couldn't envision their loss, but I could try and 'be there' to provide, at least, a loving presence for their great loss. Many other family and friends surrounded us with God's love and a much-needed 'village' support system in the wake of a wife and a mom's passing. The hymn that was my companion during the final months of Charlotte's life and an ongoing source of grace was 'It Is Well with My Soul.' I sang that hymn and read those words lots of times, remembering 'when sorrows like sea billows roll,' that it can be rocky and rough on the outside but tranquil and well on the inside. I learned about that hymn while in basic training for becoming a chaplain in the army in 1978. How fortunate I was to hear the grace and goodness of God come back to me, again and again, in those blessed words. Yes, grace was present 'when sorrows like sea billows roll.' Grace provided the 'Sweet' for the phrase 'Sweet Sorrow.'

Church and Ministry

21

Grace in Simple Phone Calls

I was looking at my cell phone caller ID. Again, it was Lois Froebel. Often, she called to inform me – and many others - of situations in our former congregation involving people with special needs or perhaps telling me that someone had died. Lois has been a dear and close friend from a congregation I served over forty years ago in Brooklyn Park, Minnesota. She is an energetic, caring, funny lady of 90+ years. We love her dearly and so appreciate her calls every time. Lois lost her husband, Chuck, about twelve years ago and, while missing him dearly, has used her days since to bless folks in many ways. Her calling to people to let them know what's happening in the lives of others is nothing short of graciousness. She makes between five to ten calls every day in this ministry of caring. Her name is Lois, but her (phone) 'calling' is grace - God's grace. Here it comes: "Hi Lois, what's happening?" My heart is warmed.

22

Grace in Half-Set Jello

Often, I am involved in conversations that revolve around difficult issues. Not all conversations require a 'yes' or 'no,' but stating one's belief or opinion is where conversations often go. I am thinking just now of a particular conversation that I had with our director of music, our senior choir director, at Grace Lutheran Church. I don't remember the issue; it was only a comment Steve made in that conversation, which I thoroughly enjoyed and have remembered ever since. Describing how he saw himself his posture about many things, he said, "When offering an opinion, I often feel like half-set Jello." Wow, I thought, that is really being honest! How often have I been unsure of what I think? Oh, some things seem very clear, but many times it just doesn't appear black and white. Steve gave me a gift of grace that day, as he shared his own uncertainty and sometimes confusion. I now felt permission to be more honest about my uncertainty, more willing to be vulnerable and even bewildered. I told Steve that day that I preferred red Jello to green. (Too many funeral luncheons serve green Jello. I'm tired of that.) But, not tired of Steve's honesty, uncertainty and grace.

23

Grace in Loyal Partnership

Partnership is defined by Webster as, 'the state of being a partner, participation." Working in the church all those years, I often worked with colleagues, others, and partners. Together, many of us participated in serving in ministry, helping empower others to love our neighbors. Today, I remember two special ministry partners beyond the outstanding pastoral colleagues and lay staff in each parish. At Grace Lutheran Church in Apple Valley, I inherited - upon arrival - two Parish Nurses: Lois Askvig and Amy Fleser. They had specific responsibilities, such as organizing 'health activities' in the parish. The blessing I want to lift-up here is the partnership we pastor shared with these nurses in the overall care of the congregation. The awareness of needs within the congregation, such as the listening ears of compassion, the wisdom shared when advise was needed, the nursing skills regarding blood pressures or dietary requirements, and many more were always known, rarely missed. The best image I can offer here is that Amy and Lois were our pastoral partners who had their 'ears to the ground' way more than we could have, given the scope of our pastoral responsibilities, in toto. Those two multiplied our pastoral ministry many-fold, and the members of Grace were the grateful recipients. Those two multiplied the grace of God way more than the two members of our pastoral staff with 'Reverend' in front of our names. Indeed, grace in partnership.

24

Grace in the Third World

Our congregation in Apple Valley, Grace Lutheran Church, was part of an exchange program through the St. Paul Area Synod of the ELCA to visit congregations in Guatemala. Small groups of members would travel to Guatemala every eighteen months to spend a week, mostly in a small village, getting to know the people there. This was not a mission of evangelism; but rather companionship, as we were in the ministry of 'walking together.' Our presence and prayers during that time was what we brought; they knew the Gospel and were living adequately, though modestly by affluent standards. As their visitors, we often enjoyed playing with the children. We observed that the parents (far from helicoptering) often did not know where their kids were. So, we would join a group of fifteen to twenty young people in the open grass space and often do little more than kick a soccer ball or toss a frizbee. As we reflected on our time in Guatemala, many of us shared the experience of seeing multiple children playing with one soccer ball, rarely in conflict and – to our surprise – on a really low budget. These children were genuinely happy most of the time. No computers, Switch games, expensive sports equipment, or complaining. The lesson of grace for me/us was that happiness was not measured by how many toys were on the premises. Lovely children. Grace is seen within poverty.

25

Grace in the Face of Difficult Decisions

Linda Kelsey, a member of Memorial Lutheran Church in Afton, Minnesota, came up to me after worship one Sunday and wanted to talk about an idea she had for a drama that could be used in our church. Linda (and her husband Glenn) had moved back to Hudson, Wisconsin, a couple of years earlier from Hollywood, where she had been a successful actress. Linda acted in a number of television programs but was mostly known for her role as 'Billie' on the Lou Grant Show in the 1980s. On that Sunday, Linda shared her idea of creating a drama for the church: 'What Would You Do? The scenes and dialogue vacillated between real persons during the Holocaust, some who supported the Hitler regime and others who resisted. The numerous dialogues were sentences and paragraphs taken verbatim from people back then; Linda's added creative scripts invited the audience to put themselves in the place of the actors – given these most difficult times in 1930s Germany – and consider: 'What Would You Do?' The actors continued to switch roles, revealing average citizens' difficulty, dispelling the notion that decisions were black and white, evil or good. It was a dynamic, ethical, personal drama of ultimate challenge to the audience, amplifying the ambiguity of real life, then and now. Linda knew, as we all do that making decisions in relative comfort presents no problem; what about those ordinary Germans whose personal decisions could well occasion the deaths of family, friends, and neighbors? I discovered the grace that Linda attempted to offer the audience. Jolted out of our everyday apathy and unfortunate ignorance that we can slip into as middle-class Americans, we were presented the opportunity to remember and rehearse what we might do when faced with dilemmas in our own time and place. Linda's creativity was a gracious gift to Memorial Lutheran Church and the other places it showed. Thank you, Linda!

26

Grace is Contexual

I had only been in my new parish assignment (Prince of Peace Lutheran Church of Brooklyn Park, Minnesota) for a few months. It was a Saturday morning, and I showed-up at the church where the Property Committee was busily yellow striping the entire parking lot, manually. Right over there, with gloves on and a roller pad was our Senior Pastor, Erik Saxvik. He said, "Good morning, John. Great to see you here. Let me get you a roller." I paused momentarily, experiencing an identity crisis. In the seminary we were taught to not get involved in 'floors and doors,' rather let the laypeople take charge and do that. Our calling as pastors was to preach, teach, and administer the sacraments. Further, I had just come off of four years as an associate pastor, being told there to 'highly regard your calling and stick to spiritual matters.' With my identity crisis in full motion and being brand new at this call, I responded to Pastor Erik's invitation: "I, I . . . guess that wou. . . would be fine." I enjoyed painting that morning in the Fall of 1979 and learned that creating relationships and showing solidarity often begins with 'floors and doors.' Three months later, while at a church council meeting in Pastor Erik's home, I noticed (how observant of me :) that in addition to hors d'oeuvres, most everyone was sharing a drink. I don't mean lemonade or ice tea; most everyone was enjoying a mixed drink, a glass of wine or beer. Remember that earlier parish where the pastor was to 'stick to spiritual matters?' I also learned there that the pastor shouldn't even drink wine in pubic. Imagine that? The Norwegian/Hauge piety, plus memories of Moorhead's prohibition days, created that strict judgment on the pastors. But here, on a new call, in a different place, council members were not only drinking but also at a council Christmas gathering. Now I'm all confused. Later, I talked with Erik about this, and he reassured me that if I shared a drink or had a beer, I would not be losing my job or my career. I needed to learn that a few behaviors are absolutely bad (oh, for sure some are), but that experiencing grace is very contextual. Painting and drinking, both done in moderation for sure. . . all for the glory of God!

Grace in my Early Years

27

Grace is Rarely Black and White

Perhaps the single-most important force that shaped my early life was my involvement in Boy Scouting. Entering the program at age seven as a Cub Scout, I traveled upward through every rank and received most every award. While unusually young, I received the coveted rank of Eagle Scout at age thirteen, later to earn the Lutheran religious award and by age seventeen, presented the Vigil Honor award of the Order of the Arrow. Although I was active in swimming, basketball, music and student government, scouting took up most of my free time and shaped my life most significantly. Fortunately, I had a father who valued what scouting offered; my Dad was actively involved in scouting, finally receiving the Silver Beaver Award, recognizing his serious commitment for over twenty years. It was my Dad who realized that the goals of scouting for "character building, physical fitness and citizenship training" would serve his son well into the future. I will forever be grateful that I reaped the benefits of scouting.

Rarely is grace and blessing simply black or white, good or bad. Often, with gracious activity and worldly blessing comes attendant shadows. Not always, but many times there is a dark side to things wonderful, at least grey. Well, for at least three decades, the Boy Scouts of America hotly debated the issue of homosexuality, specifically whether gay persons should be allowed in leadership positions in the program. Besides the practical issues of camping and swimming and living closely together for children and adolescents, which have now mostly been resolved, there remains a wide divide between those who believe the program has room for persons in leadership with homosexual orientations and those who maintain a traditional position rejecting such. (Sadly, many in the BSA fail to understand the difference between homosexual orientation and pedophilia. One is a God-given reality not to be feared, and one is a severe psychiatric disorder that usually requires restriction and treatment.) As one who both benefited immensely from the scouting program and who understands homosexuality as an orientation and identity, not a choice, I find this conflict disturbing and difficult. I wish for scouting to practically work out the details of accepting, if not yet affirming, homosexuality, yet this apparent stand-off shows me one further shape of grace: organizations, like individuals, are imperfect. The shape of grace I see in scouting is that many things it values and encourages are so important, yet this program, like anything human, is not perfect. Time will tell, and circumstances will likely precipitate change and perhaps greater authenticity. One of grace's shapes is the recognition that often good things are neighbors to not-such-good-things. Rarely are things simply black or white. The struggle goes on. 'On my honor, I will do my best. . . ' (from the Boy Scout Oath)

28

Grace in Endings

During my freshman and junior years at Muskegon Senior High School (1964-66), I not only sang in the 60-voice Acapella Choir and the 16-voice Madrigalian group, I was also selected to be the MHS mascot, the Big Red Indian. My experience with the Indian Dance Team in the Nakida Naou Lodge #401 of the Order of the Arrow (Boy Scouts of America) prepared me for this position. The mascot attended all the pep rallies, the varsity football games and the varsity basketball games. I was one of the cheerleaders. In the year 2,000, thirty-three years after I graduated, after considerable discussion and a Board of Education decision, the Indian mascot position was retired. I understood the sensitivity and political correctness behind this decision; as early as 1967, our Dance Team was learning about – and sensitive to – the increasing pressure to have greater respect for Native American traditions, especially religious ones like the Ghost Dance from the Sioux nation in South Dakota. I didn't know then, but I have learned plenty since about the genocide of Indigenous peoples over 400 years in the Americas. The Muskegon Board of Education's decision was right; our nation's recognition of one of its original sins is now more recognized, as it always should've been. Yet, selfishly and emotionally, it was hard to see the Big Red Indian tradition at MHS be ended. Behind the end of that tradition was a grace-filled reckoning of awareness, sensitivity, and growth.

29

Grace Through Accountability

It is indeed ironic that I . . . who spent my entire professional career of ministry and Christian education focused on Dietrich Bonhoeffer, the Holocaust, and 20th century German history . . . flunked German 201 in college. I had taken a semester of German (101) during my first year of community college, and then, when transferring to Concordia College in Moorhead, Minnesota, enrolled in German 201. It was much more challenging, and going into the final exam in German 201 with a 'C' average assumed that - if I failed the final - I would still get a 'D,' and pass. Oops! Wrong assumption. I did fail the final and failed the class. Unlike high school and year one of college, I quickly learned that Concordia did not give away grades because you were nice, sincere, and showed-up for class. I needed that lessen to later succeed in the rest of my college and seminary classes. Of course, I was mad (at myself) for getting a failing grade so soon into my second year of college; when you start low, it is very hard to raise the Grade Point Average back up. German 201 (failing German 201) taught me a very important life lesson: accountability. And, I am most grateful for that lesson, even though the sound of grace was not so apparent.

30

Grace from a Professor

In preparation for becoming a pastor, I continued my education at Luther Theological Seminary in St. Paul after college. It was a wonderful education, and I could not have asked for better preparation to serve in parish ministry. During the first year, while taking an Introductory class in Old Testament (Old does not mean worn-out and useless, but rather comes before the New), the assignment was given to read 'A History of Israel' by John Bright. Numbering close to five hundred pages, it was the gold standard, the go-to book for overview and reference regarding things about ancient Israel. The seminary had pretty much given-up 'objective' testing, leaning rather into essays, interpretation, and small group dialogue. However, the upcoming assignment for this Old Testament class included an objective test on Bright's entire book. The fifty questions (if I remember correctly) were to both test our knowledge and ensure that we had, in fact, read the entire book. I read the book carefully, showed-up for class, and proceeded to take the test. I wasn't confident that I would do very well but merely hoped to pass the test. Two days later, our Professor, Dan Simundson, returned the graded test to class. "Wow," I said to myself. "This is probably the first time in my life that I received a grade of 55%, which was clearly failing." I quickly turned over the test on my desk and attentively began listening to Dr. Simundson's lecture on the ancient Israelites, who I also observed failed a few times. After class, I sheepishly approached the professor, commenting on my less-than stellar grade on the test. He said, "Well, why don't you reread the book and then re-take the test. I bet you will pass it then." I knew myself well enough, and offered what I thought to be a reasonable explanation and possible plan: "Dr. Simundson, I believe in accountability and testing. I fear that I could read that text ten more times and would not do much better. I have always had trouble with these kinds of objective tests" He said, "OK. Read it again, and we'll call it good." I said, "I really appreciate that. Thank you." Since those seminary days, at about age forty, I was diagnosed with Attention Deficit with Hyperactivity Disorder (ADHA). Retaining that amount of historical detail (John Bright's A History of Israel) was nearly impossible for me, even though I could grasp the bigger picture well. Dr. Simundson, even before ADHD was in the psychiatric DSM, acted graciously, and I was really grateful. I knew the standard; I expected him to hold a tight line. I never had another objective test during those four years of graduate theological education, and I became a pastor and a university adjunct instructor. The shape of this grace came in the understanding of a professor.

31

Grace in Quiet Reprimand

I can remember the Saturday morning like yesterday. It was a summer Saturday in 1959. The night before, I and two other friends had camped in our backyard. Rod, Mickey and I probably laid awake telling stories until midnight. It was about 3:00 AM when Rod, a couple of years older and liking to stir things up, woke Mickey and me up with the brilliant idea of heading down the alley toward Eddie Edson's house. Eddie had a large garden, with mostly vegetables and fruits, and many of those were ripe and ready to pick. Rod's less-than-brilliant idea was for us to pick some of Eddie's tomatoes and throw them on the back of Eddie's house. Being the Boy Scout I was, I had serious reservations, but I also succumbed to the peer pressure and went along with the prank. Fast forward to the next morning. We woke up, took down the tent, brought our sleeping bags into the house, and carried-on, as if nothing had happened. About 11:00 AM, my Dad came outside to the porch stoop on which I was sitting and said, "Eddie Edson wants to talk with you and the boys. He's coming here in about ten minutes." Oh crap! My Dad remained calm. Eddie arrived at 11:15 AM, and I cannot today remember exactly what Eddie said to me. After he left, my Dad asked, "What did Eddie want to talk about?" (Of course, my Dad knew already) I told my Dad the whole story, and it surprised me that he didn't dish-out some harsh consequences. Rather, he said, "Did you learn your lesson?" What else could a scared ten-year old say when immanent punishment or death seemed more unlikely if my answer was, "You bet I did!" I remember my Dad said very little, almost nothing. I never forgot his silence and what I assumed to be his understanding: this kind of thing is not what Johnny would normally do. He also, I later learned, factored in Rod's proclivity for mischievous activity, and he thought I would not likely do such a thing again. I remember later discussing with both of my parents why destroying Eddie's garden vegetables was so unkind since he worked so hard to grow them. I learned about grace, in part, from my Dad's quiet reprimand regarding our criminal activity.

Therapy and Counseling

32

Grace in the Challenge of ADHD

I was in my forties when a psychotherapist observed that one of the things I might be struggling with was Attention Deficit Disorder (ADHD). While this disorder had been an identifiable category in the Diagnostic & Statistical Manual of Psychiatric Disorders (DSM) for some years, it was not something I had learned about nor thought of as something I might be struggling with. My lack of focus, my inability to memorize things (remember the 55% on my seminary test?), and my difficulty keeping things in order were things I could trace back to my childhood; now it was helpful to see that these challenges were not simply a matter of my having a lower IQ or simple disinterest. In fact, there were neurological factors that made such normal activities difficult. (I didn't struggle with the hyperactivity often associated with this disorder that makes it ADHD.) Following this diagnosis and recognition led to embracing new ways of handling things. First, one can take certain medication that assists the brain synapses to improve focus, memory, and order. Second, and actually more long-lasting and helpful, were the tricks I came to use that dramatically improved my performance and significantly helped my relationships. Things like making lists and bullet-pointing assignments and asking myself questions along the way . . . these all helped me live more productively and relate more responsibly. How might one find grace in such a life challenge? Isn't it simply a deficit that one identifies and then works with? In the years since that initial diagnosis, I have often thought about how this challenge of ADHD might also be a blessing. Is it simply trying to make lemonade out of a lemon? Perhaps. Accompanying my disorder was a desire to learn and become fully educated. In college, I chose to major in philosophy and religion. Unbeknownst to me then was the fact that critical thinking, deeper reflection and interpersonal relationships were things ADHD people can have some success with. Memorizing drugs and the periodic table of elements, and mastering the phyla of mammals or classification of plants would never ever come easy. While medicine and physical chemistry would not be careers I would likely succeed at, theology, ministry, and counseling could be. And the rest is history. . . In addition to the joy I came to experience in Christian ministry, college teaching, and military chaplaincy (all things people with ADHD can do very well), I came to thank God for the graciousness that was my lot, and eventually my strength, by not being able to memorize scripture and remember every detail of the day. I was never able to use scripture as a weapon in conversation, nor was I able to flaunt how perfect my organization skills were. Grace was often experienced – and then expressed - in broken, imperfect ways, sharing the imperfection of life with other imperfect people. While I think I learned and could express some wisdom and compassion, God's gift of an ADHD disorder never allowed me to arrogantly use what I knew to control or hurt other people. One Sunday, as worship ended, a mom came through the line and thanked me profusely for the sermon in which I had shared my challenge with ADHD. She told me her young son also had that, and that it was encouraging and hopeful for her to hear that someone else with that had 'made something of their life.' Grace again . . .

33

Grace in Shared Brokenness

In 1986, I learned about a support group called Adult Children of Alcoholics (ACOA). I knew of Alcoholics Anonymous and Alanon, since I came from an (extended) alcoholic environment growing-up. It was while paying good money for an excellent therapist that Adult Children of Alcoholics was recommended to me, since recognizable, 'garden variety' symptoms of co-dependence, repressed anger and emotional denial were obvious pieces of my earlier and present life. Of course, my first reaction was, "I don't see why meeting with people, who've come from alcoholic families, would be of help to me." But, Alan, my therapist, pressed hard, providing me the calendar of days and times of some local meetings, and off to my first ACOA group on a Tuesday at noon I went. Entering the smoke-filled room was uncomfortable and embarrassing, and I certainly didn't want to appear like I was one of them. Especially since I was a Lutheran pastor, I felt out-of-place and wasn't even sure how to introduce myself. The fundamental reality that I, like each of them, was a broken person didn't cross my mind at that time. I remember there being about eight people sitting in a circle of chairs, mostly women with one man. I later learned that the other man in the group was also a Lutheran pastor; that helped a little. I assumed that everyone there was trying to improve, and soon I learned a fundamental ground rule: everyone attending was to be as honest as possible. What a novel idea. The group members were very friendly and welcoming. Yet, in spite of that, I really felt uneasy. Defensive people feel that way. As a pastor, I was usually the one in charge, the one with answers, and expected to be the one who had it all together. Here, I joined the ranks of broken human beings who all somehow reached the bottom and were hoping for a better life ahead. I looked around, wondering who the leader was. Quickly, after brief introductions, one person explained the process, and said that there is no one leader. And around we went, telling our stories, that is, why we were there and what we hoped to accomplish. When they got to me, I said, "Hi. I'm John . . ." They responded, "Hello, John. Welcome. We are glad you came today." I think at this first meeting, I attempted to share how good a person I was, how successful a pastor I had become and that I didn't even know exactly what I had to discover. Soon into the go-around, it became clear that the seasoned members of the group had pretty insightful bullshit barometers and could see through any self-adjulation and superficial chatter. Maybe I wasn't in the right group? Had my therapist misjudged my needs and dysfunctions? Fast forward . . . a few weeks, and probably months, it became obvious that I was very much in the right group, did have things to learn, and had joined a segment of humanity that shared my family of origin brokenness, those not-so-helpful ways of coping. These were people who could genuinely support me in my pain and growth. God's goodness came to me as I learned over a two-year period, with a most unlikely group of people, that grace is often known in our shared brokenness. There, I came to know God's grace in one woman's domestic abuse, another's loss of a child, and still another's controlling behavior to cover deep shame and insecurity. Wow. Here was a group of folks that not only needed grace, but provided grace . . . to even me, someone who thought he had it all together.

34

Grace Needed in Acknowledgement

It happened many months into psychotherapy, when my counselor gently asked me to share what conflicts were like between my wife and me. Because such recollection surfaced pain and failure, I did everything I could to simply conceptualize - stay in my head - and objectively describe the dynamics when she and I would get into conflict. I described how I wanted to be anywhere in the world except there and that, most often, she was aggressive in those exchanges. While I always tried to defend myself and back her off, I really didn't see anyway to get beyond our impasse in conflict except to suggest that she calm down and stop attacking me. Simple enough. It was then that Alan, my therapist, volunteered to interpret what he saw happening, asking me to entertain his ideas as perhaps helpful. Alan wondered if how I was responding to my wife's aggressive confrontation (regardless of the issue) resembled my behavior growing up. He asked if 'going into a corner' was how I handled conflict growing up in my childhood home. Whether physically or emotionally, was my non-engagement a way of protecting myself from attack? And then came the insightful moment when Alan asked, "Although as a child you needed to emotionally retreat into a corner to protect yourself, or so you thought, perhaps as an adult, you can stay engaged and fight it out? You are not that child you were then." In the painful acknowledgment of a pattern learned early in life, to hide and protect myself, it was now, in a marriage where my partner needed someone with whom to spar, came grace and a life-giving change I never could've discovered on my own. I did practice staying engaged, experimenting with conflict resolution, and working on something that was very unfamiliar to me, even painful. I was no longer that young, shy, and vulnerable child; I could choose as an adult to behave differently. I did. . . and my relationship with my wife changed for the better. Thank you, Alan, for your insight; thank you, God, for using painful acknowledgment as a means of grace.

# Chaplaincy and the Military

35

Grace in Collegiality

It was the Fall of 2004 when my son, Bryan, asked if I might be interested in serving as a Burnsville Police chaplain. He had been an officer with that department for a year and learned that they were in need of an additional chaplain. I agreed, interviewed with Chief Bob Hawkins and, after the proper background check, was sworn-in shortly after. There are usually six chaplains in that group, and they serve both the police and fire departments in the city of Burnsville, Minnesota. Call-outs most often are for death notifications to families, ministry related to suicides, and fires in multi-family dwellings. Additionally, the chaplains offer pastoral care for the police and fire personnel, especially when those persons are having emotional and relational challenges and crises. To nurture positive relations among the chaplains and the police/fire leadership, the Burnsville chaplains gather every Friday morning at 9:00 AM in a local Rise and Wine coffee shop on Nicollet Avenue for briefings and sharing with one another about incident call-outs. Often, the fire and police chiefs attend, along with their assistants and captains. Over the years, our friendships have deepened and the collegiality felt is nothing short of grace. I look forward to these weekly gatherings as part of my spiritual, mental, and relational health. It's a shape of grace for me. . . in, with and under every kind of conversation. Thanks Mark, Tom, John, Jim, Roger, Reese, Jill, and Trent.

36

Grace under Tears

On the morning of February 18, 2024, at about 5:52 AM, I was called by Captain Don Stenger of the Burnsville Police Department to gather the chaplains because four officers had been shot earlier that morning. Arriving at the Police department twenty minutes later, I was dispatched to the Hennepin County Medical Center in downtown Minneapolis. There I was escorted by Minneapolis officers to our Burnsville Chief, Tanya Schwartz, who ushered me to the bedside of one of the officers who had been shot but was expected to live. There, we listened and prayed and felt deep gratitude for the survival of Adam yet grief for the three who didn't. The entire situation, for days to come, was filled with grief and anger and sadness, as the wider community dealt with an incredibly painful loss. Tears flowed profusely, including those of my son, Bryan, who was as an investigator also involved in handling this tragedy. Of course, it was a relief that morning to know that our son was OK, but our relief was complicated because of the young officers who died. I was so moved by the steady flow of tears down the cheeks of Chief Tanya, who was grappling with the death of two of her officers and one paramedic, and the injury of one more. She seemed like a mother grieving the death of her children. So often, extremely sad situations cause people, especially men, to lock-up and have a 'stiff upper lip.' I understand that. But, in Chief Tanya's tears, the entire department – and all of us around – were given permission, even grace, to experience and express the depth of our pain and the greatness of our loss. Thank you, Chief.

67

37

Grace in Honesty

It was a hot August afternoon on a southern exposure hillside at Fort McCoy, Wisconsin. I was the chaplain for the Support Battalion of the 205th Brigade of the 6th Infantry Division for our two-week summer camp, making drop-in visits to soldiers on an afternoon field exercise. I had to shield the sun from my face as I approached a heavy-set, seasoned soldier sitting on the ground at the base of an old oak tree. As I got closer, I could see Sergeant Miller in tears, with his arms folded and resting on his knees. He knew by my insignia that I was the chaplain, and I think we had spoken with each other earlier in the week. I asked, "What's goin' on, Sergeant?" While wiping away tears, he embarrassingly said, "I don't know. I just can't seem to move beyond my past." I said, "Can you tell me about that?" SST Miller proceeded to share with me some stories about his service time in the 1970s when he was in Vietnam. Thinking that going a little deeper would help in his healing, I asked if he had killed anyone. He responded, "Yes, I did." I thought, "Now we are getting somewhere." But, after an uncomfortable pause of a minute or two, he continued, "But that wasn't the worst part." I said, "Tell me more." He shared, in a spirit of confession (which is where we chaplains often found ourselves), that simply killing a Viet Cong soldier would be something he thinks he could learn to live with. He went on, "It wasn't just killing someone that haunts me. What's so hard to deal with is that I enjoyed it!" As a military chaplain, I had heard plenty of war-time stories, but this twist on things was new. SST Miller went on to describe how making such killing into a game with his comrades was the only way they could survive the Hell - and boredom - of Viet Nam. For this, he felt terribly guilty, and because of this, he could not move on. This kind of guilt was not a simple thing to deal with, as if it was less horrendous because he was commanded to do it. No, carrying - out orders was one thing; enjoying something that is clearly against God's will and human sensitivity was another. As a chaplain, it was my duty not to use trite words that diminished the wrong that was done; his 'enjoyment,' not his killing, was the issue. In the shadow of his honesty, the grace required was God's radical grace, which moves one beyond all evil. We talked more and needed to feel God's grace that covered not mere incidental mistakes but radical sin. Diminishing the depth of his evil thoughts was not what would lead to healing; amplifying the grace of God, as we hear in the words and deeds of Jesus and other Rabbis and Imams, is what heals. Only brutal honesty paves the way for experiencing grace.

38

Grace in My Father-in-Law's Pain

James was only twenty-three years old when he answered the call to serve in the United States Army for the last two years of World War II. James, my father-in-law, saw what no human being, not least a young man barely out of his teens, should ever have to see. Week after week, he experienced the bloody deaths of friends and foes, fellow American soldiers as well as Italian infantry and later members of the German Wehrmacht. Few in the armed forces during WWII escaped the trauma which haunted James for the rest of his life. Now, we call it Post Traumatic Stress Disorder (PTSD). Then, it was just doing your duty. I was honored to have my father-in-law share something of his (repressed) pain from combat trauma fifty years earlier since he rarely did, and few in the family knew the depth of his agony. You see, James found a way to cope in the years after 1945. His coping was often painful for his wife, Alfreda, and their four children, Jerry, Becky, Patty (my wife), and Jeff. One can't aestheticize emotional pain with alcohol and not have those around suffer from the 'coping.' My father-in-law died of cancer in 1995, exactly fifty years after he returned from military service in Europe. In those fifty years, James tried his level best to simply live, earn a decent wage, and support his family. Sadly, the effects of his coping played out in brokenness and pain for those closest to him. Is there grace to be found in my father-in-law's life? There certainly was nothing gracious about the trauma he experienced in the desert of North Africa, the trenches of Italy, the farm lands of southern Germany, nor - for that matter - in the consumption of alcohol that occurred regularly at the local VFW with his cronies in the 1950's, 60's and 70's. Likewise, grace would not be a word to describe James' critical and condescending words to the ones he loved. So what shape did grace take as the after-effects of the war played out in his life? I see grace in the fifty years that his wife, my mother-in-law, stood by his side, painfully enduring abusive talk and actions. I see grace in his children who keep going in life in-spite of their own painful memories. I see grace in the forgiveness that came forth for James in his final days. I see grace in the tears I shed simply listening to his story. The shape of grace that I have seen then and now is the love, kindness, forgiveness and reconciliation that has taken place in-spite of the Hell that war created for James. And, one shape of grace that I trust is the loving arms of Jesus who, in 1995, welcomed this broken man into the heavenly realm, where smiles and hugs and forgiveness and joy will be the order of the day, not bullets, howitzers, violence, alcohol and abuse. One of the shapes that grace has taken - and will take in eternity - is in healing the brokenness of wartime trauma.

Bible and Theology

39

Grace and Biblical Errancy

Somewhere in high school, I was told that the Bible was the 'inerrant, infallible Word of God.' I ran with that idea, and it was reinforced in college when I uncritically accepted the notion of 'Propositional Revelation' propagated by Francis Schaeffer (mentioned in my Preface). Briefly, 'inerrant, infallible' is a belief that the ideas and theology written in the sixty-six canonical Christian Bible books are without error and to be completely accepted de facto. Propositional revelation accepts that some of the geographical and historical detail might be inaccurate (after all, it was written by people), but that the propositions are infallible. Yes, these books were written by people, but the Spirit of God somehow insured that the ideas/propositions were exactly as God intended. While I was in the seminary, the Historical Critical Method of biblical study, both higher and lower criticism, came to be the way I then - and now - read the scriptures. The Historical Critical Method makes use of social, literary and contextual materials to understand what an author likely knew - and didn't know - and finally meant when composing the text. This ultimately means that context and chronology and ideas and (even) theology experienced and expressed back then need to be critically examined in light of all we can know. That is, the words, the ideas and the beliefs of persons two and three millennia ago cannot be uncritically called the 'inerrant, infallible Word of God,' if that means accurate in absolutely every way. What maturity of faith and growth in understanding has come to mean, for me, is that God has always used imperfect, improbable, unlikely persons, places and events to reveal Godself. Jacob, Israel, Jeremiah, Job, Jesus, Paul, Mother Therese, even the Bible, are imperfect vessels that can still reveal something of God's grace and purpose. It appears as though God has freely chosen to express Godself through very human, broken, imperfect people and events. I suppose the challenge for the Church, and all people who look to the Bible for guidance, support and truth, is to discover just what verses and ideas are God's and what experiences and thoughts are those of (merely?) the Biblical authors. It is always easier to simply assume every word, verse, and idea in the Bible came directly from God; this literalism is the essence of Fundamentalism. More difficult is the hard work of reading, contemplating, and deciding what verses meant then and how they might be relevant for us today. Risky? Perhaps, but I – for one – have come to see that I have no other choice. I have found God's grace even in the Bible's errors. It's the way God conducts business with me.

40

Grace in Re-interpretation

After many years of questioning and stumbling on John 14:6 in the New Testament, I decided to bring together my faith, my education, and my desire to make sense of this most challenging verse in the Gospel of John. John 14:6 is one of the most polarizing/exclusive verses in the New Testament: "Jesus said to him, 'I am the way, and the truth and the life. No one comes to the Father, except through me." (NRSV) This verse, but not only this verse (cf. Acts 4:12 & Hebrews 8:13), seems to clearly state that Jesus supersedes all other ways of people knowing truthfully – and relating ultimately – to God. While this verse has served to motivate countless followers of Jesus over twenty centuries to dedicate their lives to help proselytize every other human being on the planet, it has also served to allow – if not encourage – rejection, abuse, and even genocide of those persons not affirming the 'salvation exclusive' message of the Church. Perhaps it is the result of the world becoming smaller and people having greater contact with persons/religions quite different than their own that a re-examination of this verse seems in order. For sure, John 14:1-5, the verses immediately preceding 14:6, were meant to offer pastoral comfort for the anxious disciples about their uncertain future. Jesus assures them that the 'way' of God, known through the Torah, is his way, that the 'truth' he speaks is of God's truth, and the 'life' to which he has given witness is eternal. However, verse six – with its exclusive, even arrogant, emphasis – has led to conclusions that Jesus would not likely have drawn. Scholars are in general agreement that the Gospel of John was composed in the last decade of the First century. At that time, many of the followers of Jesus – who were primarily Jews - were struggling to know how their life-enriching experience of Jesus related to their being Jews, that is, God's covenant people. As each group, Jews and the followers of Jesus, worked to know their place in God's economy of salvation, their exchanges often became adversarial, even hostile. This competitive environment related to who – of these two groups – was to be the official inheritor of God's covenant: Torah observant Jews or the followers of Jesus? In this competitive environment where communal identity was at stake, we can locate and understand the urgency and exclusivity of John's proposal that Jesus is the only way, truth, and life, and how anyone not following this way of Jesus cannot know God. John wrote those words, which summarize his conviction about Jesus' exclusive access to the Father. However, such exclusive language does not resonate with the more inclusive understanding of God we know about Jews and Judaism; and we must never forget that, at the beginning and ending of every day, Jesus was a Jew! Again, it is understandable that John believed Jesus began a new chapter in Israel's history, and that access to God involved entering through the life, death, and resurrection of Jesus. John's life was dramatically changed through his encounter with Jesus, and his passion to make that experience available to all others follows from that passion. It does not make sense for us to assign that exclusiveness to Jesus, a Jew who knew that there was not just one way to access and know God. John's exclusive experience of Jesus need not (should not?) be a necessary formula for everyone in the future who follows Jesus. We are given permission to ask such important questions about the content of the Gospels (Matthew, Mark, Luke, and John), because each of these four are Gospels 'according to . . . ' those four persons/communities. We have come to know that each of the authors placed their own stamp and interpretation on their understanding of the life, death, and resurrection of Jesus. And so, we are honoring John by retaining his words based on his experience and honoring Jesus by remembering his Jewish faith and inclusive experience. A possible reconstruction of this verse by me would look like this: 'I have shown you the way, the truth, and life. To know God is to follow this way, understand this truth, and live this life.' (The original NRSV should be reverently placed in the footnotes, encouraging readers to reflect on how those times differed from ours.) In suggesting such a re-interpretation, my goal has been to lift-up the graciousness and inclusivity we know in Jesus while honoring the context of John's original experience and words. In fact, I believe that grace is alive in re-interpretation; static, legalistic, literal repetition of ancient texts feels more like stagnation and death.

41

Grace Simultaneous with Sin

The life and legacy of Martin Luther have been explained and expounded in multiple ways, ranging from biographical details to his profound, world-changing theology. I was raised a Lutheran long before I even knew who this man was or what his influence and legacy amounted to. In college - then in the seminary - I learned of his Catholic upbringing, his spiritual struggles, his priesthood, his academic career, his conflict with the Roman Catholic Church, and finally, his painful excommunication from the church. (Recently, I gifted Augsburg University's religion department, for whom I worked eighteen years, with a 1739 edition of Luther's Collected Works in German that I had been given many years earlier but now had no need of.) Over the years, I learned that Martin Luther had been extremely influential in the lives of philosopher/author Sören Kierkegaard and pastor/theologian Dietrich Bonhoeffer. While Luther scholars may differ on what Luther's most significant offering was to the Church and the world, one offering most would agree on is Martin Luther's (re)discovery of the centrality of grace displayed in the life and death of Jesus. Grace is understood to be the unconditional love/embrace/acceptance of every human being by God, forever dethroning human attempts to be justified - or made right with God - by efforts of their own. Romans 1:16 could well sum-up Luther's notion of grace: "For I am not ashamed of the gospel; it is the power of God for salvation to everyone who has faith, to the Jew first and also to the Greek." At the same time, grace has always been de jure central to the Church's proclamation (even if, at times, in a distorted form), de facto virtually every generation and every tradition of Christianity succumbed to human temptation at self-righteousness and self-justification. Luther emphasized and insisted on grace as the fundamental, absolute, and never-to-be-compromised essence of the Church's life and the ultimate Word of God, above all other words. Thus far, Martin Luther's positive legacy and world-changing (re)discovery! As Luther neared the end of his life, his conflict with the Roman Catholic hierarchy and his frustration with anyone who failed to embrace God's unconditional grace, which he so wonderfully came to know, created a degree of cynicism and even contempt. This negativity found expression in several ways, not least in his 1543 essay, 'On the Jews and their Lies.' In that time, his frustration took the shape of theological supersession, bordering on physical abuse of the Jews because of their recalcitrance about - if not total rejection of - the Gospel, that is, the Christian understanding of the grace of God. Luther, in the pages of this essay, encourages attitudes and actions against Jewish people that the Nazis later employed to abuse and ultimately to attempt the extermination of the Jews of Europe (the Holocaust). In 1994, as part of my/our labors on the ELCA Consultative Panel for Lutheran-Jewish Relations, I was honored to be one of the co-authors of a 'Declaration of the Evangelical Lutheran Church in America to the Jewish Community,' a statement of repudiation of Luther's nasty, anti-Judaic diatribes, especially his 1543 essay. This historic statement was received by the Jewish community with great gratitude, and now is included in the permanent exhibit and on display in the United States Holocaust Memorial Museum in Washington, DC. One take away . . . is that our sainted Martin Luther was also a blemished human being. Yes, we need to claim the grace of God that he so nobly fought to preserve in evaluating his life. Yes, too, his inexcusable and penultimate words disparaging Jews and Judaism must be named for what they were. Beyond and beside Luther's misbehavior, the world has been blessed by his powerful grasp of grace.

42

Grace in the Irony of Martyrdom

On April 9, 1945, pastor, theologian, and Christian martyr Dietrich Bonhoeffer was murdered by the Nazis for his complicity in the plot to assassinate Adolf Hitler. Bonhoeffer was only thirty-nine years old, yet his legacy remains an inspiration: his tragic martyrdom, his authentic life, his voluminous writings, and his credible Christian faith continue to draw people in who seek an example of faith under fire, life in the face of death. I first encountered the life and theology of Dietrich Bonhoeffer while a college student at Concordia. An independent study there with Dr. James Hofrenning inspired me to focus later on the legacy of Dietrich Bonhoeffer at the seminary, and later become involved in the International Bonhoeffer Society. Meeting annually with the American Academy of Religion, that Society involvement put me in touch with scholars around the States and the world who were dedicated to perpetuating Bonhoeffer's legacy. In that academic effort, I spent time in Germany and met several of Bonhoeffer's family and colleagues in the Confessing Church. This pursuit also led to encounters in East Germany before the Fall of the Berlin Wall, and South Africa in their labor to dismantle apartheid. Editing the Society Newsletter, then serving on the board as Vice-President, and finally being President provided many opportunities for me to grow in my theological and historical knowledge of Europe – specifically Germany – during the Holocaust. Especially Bonhoeffer's later reflections on such things as the 'World Come of Age,' 'Religionless

Christianity,' and 'Responsibility' have deepened my own faith and inspired greater involvement in Jewish-Christian relations and interfaith conversation. Bonhoeffer has been my theological 'conversation partner' for almost six decades. The grace of God, like the grace of Christ's body - the Church - has expanded exponentially for me because of the gracious – yet tragic – witness of Dietrich Bonhoeffer. Bonhoeffer once quoted the Early Church Father Tertullian, who, in his Apologetics, coined the phrase, "The blood of the martyrs is the seed of the Church." For Bonhoeffer, grace was beautiful but never cheap; in fact, he coined the phrase 'Costly Grace' when speaking of God's sacrifice and our challenge in following Jesus. There are many lenses through which we see the hand of God, many vessels from which God's blessings are poured out upon us. Dietrich Bonhoeffer's life and legacy have been primary lenses and vessels for me.

43

Grace in Gentle Correction

My professional life of Lutheran ministry over forty-four years included many blessed experiences in our churches and communities. My greatest interest – and hence the largest amount of time spent – on the periphery of the ministry was that of the International Bonhoeffer Society. Having done Master's level graduate work on the legacy of Bonhoeffer between 1978-82, I was very fortunate to become acquainted with members of Bonhoeffer's family in Germany and many of his students in the Confessing Church. We hosted some of these students and their spouses in their 70s by arranging places for them to speak in the United States. These included persons like Werner Koch with his wife, Deta; Eberhard Bethge with his wife, Renate; and Wolf-Dieter Zimmermann with his wife, Friederike. During Dieter and Friederike's visit in about 1985, we gathered our family around the dinner table one evening and prayed a blessing before eating. 'Come, Lord Jesus, be our guest, and let these gifts to us be blessed.' When we finished praying, and before passing the roast beef and mashed potatoes, Dieter said, "You know, in Germany, during my time with Bonhoeffer, we were told not to pray that prayer." Seriously, I thought? Wanting to justify our reason for using it, I said, "You know, of course, Dieter, that 'your' Martin Luther composed that prayer?" He said, "Oh, yes, he did write that prayer. However, Dietrich Bonhoeffer taught us in the Confessing Church seminary at Finkenwalde that we should not be inviting Jesus to our table, but that he invites us to his table."

Oooo . . . Kkkk. There you have it. Dieter mildly 'corrected' or critiqued something we did; yet it was a powerful, gracious theological modification that I have never forgotten. Accepting his critique inspired me to write a family prayer that was Christ-centered and other-focused: 'Thanks we give to God above, for this bread this sign of love. That our words and loving deeds help bring comfort and help feed. Bless us Lord that we may be 'Christ for others' serving Thee. Amen.' Grace experienced even in correction. I think Dieter (and Bonhoeffer) was right.

44

Grace and Broader Life Perspective

It was a mid-November afternoon when I scheduled a visit with a person I knew only through his writings. I was in Boston for an annual meeting of the American Academy of Religion in 2015. In preparation for introducing Jim Carroll at our evening banquet program, I wanted to meet him ahead and get to know him. So, in the lobby of our hotel that afternoon, we met and shared something of our life journeys. James Carroll is a Catholic priest and a prolific writer, with several New York Times best-selling books to his credit (Constantine's Sword, for one). Now in his 70s, he was reflecting on his life journey, and he graciously listened to my reflections as a 66-year-old. Feeling some frustration and wondering if anything we have said or done over the years has had any lasting effect, I asked how he thinks about all that he has done and whether he feels it has made much difference in the world. In a wise and sage manner, he calmly said to me something that I needed to hear and will hopefully never forget: Jim Carroll said, "I've come to believe that the change we believe needs to happen in the world, and we've dedicated our lives to, is multi-generational. It may only happen after many years have passed." I needed to hear that gracious and humble acknowledgment of the value of our individual contributions. Thank you, Father Jim, for helping provide broader perspective to my life and labors that November afternoon. I needed, and here felt, the grace of God in a Boson hotel lobby.

Pain, Grief and Embarrassment

45

Grace Transforming Hatred into Reconciliation

It was on my every-six-year sabbatical from ministry in the summer of 2010, when I was in Memphis, Tennessee, that I received a phone call from my associate pastor, Therese, back in Apple Valley. She said, "The front of our church and the church sign were vandalized last night." I responded, as we often do, "You are kidding." "No," she went on to say, "The main sign and the banner we had placed on the highway side of the building were spray painted red with symbols of the Aryan Nation, the Star of David, and the letters 'FU.'" The 6 by 14' sign we had created and placed on the side of the building was to 'Remember Darfur' and the genocide occurring, a tragedy already taking almost a quarter million lives. On the 'Save Darfur' sign were the names of other genocides printed there to remind people passing by that we can prevent more killing, especially since we know from history that bystanders are part of the problem. The names printed on the sign were Auschwitz, Bosnia and Rwanda to alert people that the tragedy unfolding in Darfur right now was reminiscent of those other genocides. Also, it read, 'Help now.' The graffiti vandalizing the sign and the side of our church building was likely in response to the word 'Auschwitz.' Neo-Nazis and antisemites make graffiti statements like this, being of the mind that Americans have become too 'sympathetic' to Jewish suffering, such as encouraging awareness of Auschwitz, Anne Frank, and Holocaust memorials. While grotesque and actually illegal, such vandalism is not new, nor will it ever go completely away. About 10:00 AM that morning, a member of the community was driving by and saw the vandalism, and he decided to come into the church office. He was a sign painter and offered to repair the sign, at no cost, as an expression of his sadness and regret for such a terrible thing happening. Later that day, he returned and completely restored the church sign to its original beauty, removing the red paint from the side of the church building, and taking down the canvas sign that could not be repaired. This simple gesture of offering to remove paint (vandalism) from our sign and building surface after seeing the results of hatred and racist ignorance was a very grace-filled thing. I would call this 'transforming pain into healing, hatred into reconciliation.' Certainly, this was a shape of grace on that warm summer day in 2010.

46

Grace in Sarcasm

By 1990 I had spent a decade involved in Jewish-Christian dialogue. I had more than a handful of Jewish friends, and spent quality time with a number of Rabbis. My ongoing academic interest in the Holocaust had deepened my sensitivity to things Jewish, or so I thought. Absorbing my heart and mind in the history of the Holocaust has been, for me over five decades, my 'teshuva,' which is a Hebrew word for 'repentance or return.' For our annual Yom HaShoah (Holocaust) Remembrance, we invited either survivors or Rabbis to share something of the meaning of this historical caesura, helping us Lutherans be more informed and sensitive Christians/humans. This particular year I lined-up a Rabbi who served at the University of Minnesota's Hillel Center. He came to speak at our 8:00, 9:00, 10:00, and 11:00 AM worship services at Prince of Peace Lutheran Church in Brooklyn Park. During the first service, as part of his sermon, my discomfort began. In short, he used this invitation to a Lutheran congregation to excoriate 'us Christians' for our active and passive roles played during the Holocaust. I even remember him being rather sarcastic. Of course, I shared the congregation's discomfort, as we listened to very specific ways that Christians, theologians, pastors, and church bodies back then and there had woefully failed to defend Jews and countless others. I endured all four services, thanking him for being with us . . . yet, still upset that a guest preacher would abuse a captive audience. Did we need to hear those things? Yes. Could he have said them in a more fitting way? Perhaps. Thinking back on the day, I believe I did send him a note explaining why his presentation was not what I hoped for and even critically saying that his tone was offensive and unhelpful. I can't remember how he responded, if he did. In fact, I have since come to understand that the rawness of this topic, the pain this subject elicits, and the historic role Christians played in the Holocaust made the Rabbi's presentation very authentic. Yes, it was abrasive and created defensiveness; yet, until then – and since then – there remain volumes of denial and tons of repression about Christian complicity. So, speaking directly, honestly, even sarcastically, the Rabbi offered our congregation a sort of gracious invitation for us Christians to face history and accountability. Yes, grace – as invitation to repentance – can come packaged as judgement and accountability. Perhaps sarcasm got our attention.

47

Grace and Genocide

As part of an annual lecture exchange series in the International Bonhoeffer Society, I was part of the planning for the 2009 Ethics Lecture to be held in Minneapolis. In cooperation with Lori Brandt Hale at Augsburg University and Ellen Kennedy from the University of Minnesota's Center for Holocaust and Genocide Studies, we chose the topic of 'Genocide' and agreed that retired General Romeo Dalliaire, then a Senator from Ottawa, Canada, would be an excellent keynote speaker. Romeo Dallaire was the UN General chosen to oversee the 2,000 troops stationed in Rwanda in the Spring/Summer of 1994. His troops were assembled as security forces to 'prevent' ethnic unrest and cleansing. It was then, that Hutu militants and sympathizers accomplished the now famous genocide of 800,000+ Tutsis. Dallaire was tasked with 'keeping peace,' but he soon understood that to mean 'do nothing.' Traveling to the UN Headquarters in New York City, he appealed for more troops but failed to convince the Security Council to act and prevent the impeding slaughter. Dallaire returned to Rwanda to 'oversee' the genocide, a tragedy President Bill Clinton would later feel remorseful over, not having approved supportive US involvement. Dallaire spoke to an audience of about 500 people in Temple Israel in Minneapolis on this night. I was honored to introduce General Dallaire and a representative from the Canadian Consulate. After his hour-long presentation, which included personal references to his suicidal attempts and chemical dependency in the years following the Rwandan genocide, the General summarized his thoughts on the genocide: "I've come to the conclusion that there are those who sadly believe that some people are more important than others." Giving the General a ride back to the hotel that evening, I said to him, "Thank you so much for sharing your story and some things about your personal pain through these years." He said, "Thank you for having me. I am more healed every time I tell the story." I saw grace in the on-going slow recovery of a still very broken man.

48

Grace in the Struggle to Understand Race

I remember the religion class I was teaching at Augsburg University, a session for which I invited Ron Maye and his daughter Erin Maye Quaid. The topic was 'Religion and Race,' and having Ron and Erin there, as Black Americans, seemed only fitting. The students had prepared by reading materials about the organic relationship between race and religion, especially in the history of America. Knowing and trusting Erin and Ron, who were members of the congregation I served in Apple Valley, I asked this question (perhaps others had the same question): "How do you define or understand white privilege?" Erin said, "Let me try to address that." I asked not because I didn't believe it to be true, but because, on some level, it caused me (a Caucasian of average income who worked hard for what I have) to be defensive. Erin responded: "White privilege doesn't mean you haven't suffered or worked hard; rather, it means you haven't suffered or faced hardship because of the color of your skin." Eureka! That was a very helpful response, even one that stimulated in me little, if any, defensiveness. I experienced something of grace in a trusted friend's gentle but firm response. I don't expect nor deserve that graciousness from persons of color, who have been very negatively affected by the words and actions of people like me over many years, many decades, even centuries. I hope my future words and actions reflect my gratitude for such undeserving grace.

49

Grace and Embarrassment

In the course of wrapping-up an interfaith event a few years ago, which included over ten different faith traditions (e.g., Jewish, Muslim, B'Hai, Buddhist, Hindu, Lutheran, Methodist, Presbyterian, Roman Catholic, and Unitarian Universalist), I was introduced to a young Muslim couple. The gentleman reached out to shake my hand, and when I attempted reciprocating that familiar gesture with his wife, I learned quickly that she did not care to shake hands, rather smile and say, "How nice to meet you." While I think of myself as sometimes slow, I would like to think that I am not stupid. I thought to myself that day, "OK, I get it. When meeting Muslim women, don't offer a hand to be shaken." Lesson learned. Embarrassment registered. I will survive. Roughly two weeks later, one of our women's circles at Grace church was studying other religions; they asked for suggestions about guest speakers for their study of Islam. I quickly offered a name or two. One in particular I knew very well. Miriam Muhammed came a few weeks later, and I wanted to meet her at the door and lead her to the room where the women were meeting. As she approached me in the narthex, she reached out her arms and gave me an exuberant embrace, saying, "Pastor John, how wonderful to see you!" As you might imagine, I thought, "Now I am confused. Am I - or am I not - to shake hands or embrace Muslim women?" After a subsequent conversation with my (male) Muslim friends, I learned that all (Muslim) women do not feel the same but that knowing someone quite well changes the dynamics. Learning sometimes comes in the form of embarrassment and even confusion; grace is when we are given the chance to carry-on, to live and learn. I felt grace when others reminded me that making 'stupid' mistakes, even if sincerely done, is part of life's journey. Grace prevails.

50

Grace in Tearful Solidarity

Carl came to our church to share his story. He was a mission worker with the Seventh Day Adventist Church, the only American to stay in Rwanda when the 1994 genocide unfolded. Oh, he was commanded to leave, and he sent his wife and children out of the country for a safe haven. But Carl would not leave the people he had been serving, the Tutsis, those who were soon to be slaughtered. To abandon them would be a betrayal on the highest level for him. And so, he stayed through the duration of the hundred-day massacre in and around Kigali. Day after day he advocated for the victims, negotiating with the perpetrators, attempting to save any life, of any age, that he could. Day after day he witnessed hundreds of dead bodies in the streets, in homes, and even in some churches. And Carl did save a number of men, women, and children from the machetes of the perpetrators. And when it was all over, Carl was reunited with his family, ultimately returning to the United States. He was a different person. He was forever broken, forever hurt, and he's never stopped crying. Carl has been telling his story since 1994. But more importantly, he and his wife have been telling the story of the people of Rwanda. It has become his life mission to share the pain, agony, and humanity of both the victims and perpetrators of one of the twentieth century's most horrendous tragedies. Our congregation invited Carl to share his story. And he did.

Gathered in our sanctuary that evening were persons of all ages and experiences. I was one of those present who was forever changed. One must be very careful trying to find something good in a catastrophe so bad; one ought not to insult or violate the victims by searching for some redeeming factor, in what was for them sheer evil, base darkness, and an encounter with Hell. And so, the Rwandan genocide must always remain just that: sheer evil, base darkness . . . Hell. Yet, in Carl's telling of his story, one can perceive some shapes of grace and glimpses of God's presence. In the middle of his testimony, his tears welled-up, then tears streamed down his cheeks as memories of the slaughtered children and recollections of the massacred bodies of beautiful people flooded his brain. He paused to gain composure and then continued his story. The shape of grace that day was not in the details of the genocide, details that should always repulse us, scare Hell into us, and about which we should never feel comfortable. The shape of grace that day came in the tears of pain and gestures of compassion that Carl continued to feel, twenty some years after the trauma. Later, I was told that tears are shed every time Carl tells his story, as if to say the pain and the compassion he feels will never go away. . . as it shouldn't. One of the shapes that grace has taken - and will take in eternity - is that of tears, water shed from hearts that ache when others suffer.

I was told by my father many years ago, that whether personally
or professionally,
it is important to 'promise less and produce more.'

In that spirit, you will see that I 'promised' Fifty Shapes of Grace, and
now I am 'producing' fifty-seven!
I have intentionally added seven of my favorite Shapes that are especially
ironic. Often grace comes under the veil of irony, so see what you,
the reader thinks about these final seven.

51

Grace in the 'Other'

I am not proud of the fact that it was about 1986, at age thirty-seven and eleven years into Lutheran ministry, when I first experienced that divine 'grace' could be found in places and peoples other than the Christian tradition I grew up in and practiced. For sure, other peoples and religions spoke of God's love and mercy and forgiveness and judgement, but grace in all its truth-fulness was fundamentally and finally known in the life, death, and resurrection of Jesus Christ, as reflected in the Church's Master Narrative. I believed that without knowing and believing the grace – and salvation – gotten in Jesus Christ, one had no chance of being in on God's ultimate design for the world. (By the way, a major portion of the Church's population unfortunately, I think, still believes this.) It was in about 1986 that I met and got to know, Rabbi Barry Cytron when I invited him to come to Prince of Peace Lutheran Church in Brooklyn Park to speak about how Jews understood the Exodus event in their history. At that time, we, Lutherans at Prince of Peace, were studying the Book of Exodus and it struck me that having a Rabbi describe their understanding might be interesting. Barry came to the church, and spoke for an hour about Jewish ways of understanding the Exodus, and my friendship with Barry began. Over months, and finally years, we spent a lot of time together. I can't remember exactly when, but in between some of those get-togethers, it struck me – like a lightning bolt from heaven – that Barry understood and lived the same grace of God that I did.

Granted, he viewed the life and ministry of Jesus of Nazareth differently as a Jew, I realized that "I can no longer say that only Christians know the grace and goodness of God, and Jews (unfortunately) only know about God's wrath and condemnation, the law." Barry clearly lived under the love and goodness and kindness and acceptance of God . . . grace! And further, we both could speak about God's righteousness, wrath, condemnation and judgement of those things in the world that were contrary to God's will. As time went on, I came to know Rabbi Adam Stock-Spilker at Mount Zion in St. Paul, Rabbi Marcia Zimmerman at Temple Israel in Minneapolis, Rabbi Michael Latz at Shir Tikvah, Rabbi Norman Cohen at Beth Jacob, and Jewish laypersons like Ellen and Cheryl and Fred and Sandra and Sue and Eric. Right down the line, I continued to experience divine grace in the words, actions and beliefs of those who were clearly 'others' for the first thirty-seven years of my life. Then to boot - and learning more every year of God's sense of humor - after 911, I was challenged to learn more about Islam. If Judaism no longer held the prize for a religion based on God's law and wrath and judgement, at least Islam could remain in the clear category of 'other,' that which I was not. It was Rashed Ferdous and his wife Christina, in Rochester, Minnesota, who began opening yet another chapter in expanding my knowledge of grace. After having Rashed speak several times in my Religion 100 class at the Augsburg University satellite campus in Rochester, I began to hear how this Muslim understood the grace of God (Allah). Other concepts are important in Islam, but after learning about Rashed and Christina, Naima and Tameem and Zafar and John Emery, I realized that I was no longer able to say Christianity had a monopoly on God's grace. These Muslims, like my Jewish friends, like my Hindu and Baha'i and Sikh colleagues, knew the grace of God in the depths of their souls. These 'others' have brought even deeper dimensions and broader insights to my Christian experience of God's grace. I remain eternally grateful that my eyes were opened and my heart receptive to the super-abundance and all-pervasive reality of grace beyond my personal borders.

52

Grace under Broken Glass

It was in the Spring of 2000 that our group of forty-four pilgrims visited the Bonhoeffer Haus in Charlottenburg/Berlin. Our visit there was part of our journey to Oberammergau and the well-known Passion Play. After getting our tour group lost trying to find the Bonhoeffer Haus (I was so confident I knew how to get there because I had been there twice before), we were finally greeted at 43 Marienburger Allee by Pastor Gottfried Brezger, the chair of the Haus curatorium. Gottfried was a wonderful host and, with his assistant Knut, gave us a tour of the Haus and a (hour-long) lecture on the people and events that made the Haus famous. To further extend his hospitality, Gottfried went to the kitchen and retrieved four large water bottles to be shared with his guests. Before getting to the group, the bottles slipped out of his arms and fell, shattering the glass and spreading the water over a large area. We all rushed to help him clean it up, but Gottfried was so embarrassed. He was extremely gracious, and we did all we could to ease his discomfort. We were there to learn about the gracious and sacrificial love of Dietrich Bonhoeffer; it was in the gestures and embarrassment of our host that we experienced grace in another way: under broken glass. At least the Haus floor got washed.

53

Grace in a Faux Pas

It happened only once in 45 years, but it happened. Pastor Andrea and I were co-officiating the baptism of an infant on a Sunday morning. I agreed to speak the important words of sacred scripture and the blessed sacrament in our Lutheran Book of Worship, and Andrea agreed to 'water the baby.' (In our tradition, we usually sprinkle - not immerse - the person being baptized with water.) As part of the liturgy of baptism, the lines being read necessitate inserting 'he' or 'she' or 'they' as needed to make the sacrament more personal. I thought I was faithfully doing my part by saying, "Bring him to worship and teach him the Lord's Prayer, the Apostle's Creed, and the Ten Commandments." Andrea proceeded to do her part, bringing the child close to the water and sprinkling water on the forehead. I thought, "Another beautiful baptism on a beautiful day, here in the life of Logan Lynn's family." Returning to our pastors' pew in the front of the sanctuary, Pastor Andrea leaned over and quietly said, "Did you not know that Logan is a girl?" "What!" I exclaimed. "You have got to be kidding." Andrea said, "Did you not see the pink ribbon on HER head?" Oi vey. Feeling like an idiot, I immediately beelined to the family when worship had ended, embarrassingly apologizing for my blunder. Logan's Mom, Jenny, was most gracious, but how could she be? I just baptized her daughter as a son! Several years after this blunder, I saw Jenny in a public place and reiterated my apology. She again graciously said, "No problem." I said, "I hope he - I mean she -

is growing-up to be a fine individual, no thanks to her pastor's faux pas. Jenny's words of grace were more powerful than she will ever know. In the future, Pastor John, watch the color of the ribbon!

54

Grace in Political Irony

I remember the day exactly: October 25, 2023. It was the day our US House of Representatives was choosing their new Speaker. Each representative needed to stand and register their vote for which member should become the new leader. Our representative and friend, Angie Craig of Minnesota, stood-up to declare her choice. She confidently stood and said: "Today I want to wish my wife, Cheryl, a happy anniversary, and I vote for Hakeem Jeffers to be Speaker of the House." Now, for a little more context. Angie and Cheryl are in a same gender marriage. In the House that day, and soon to become the next Speaker, was Representative Mike Johnson of Louisiana's Fourth District. Representative Johnson is a very conservative politician and far from affirming same-gender relationships. Not sure that he celebrated the marriage of Angie and Cheryl that day. The next day, Angie introduced me as I prayed for the House session on October 26 at 10:00 AM. The irony ran deep as I prayed – in part - about 'affirming the complexity of gender,' after which Angie introduced me, both of us standing right in front of the new Speaker, Mike Johnson. Irony and grace often go hand-in-hand. Thank you, Angie, for your deep understanding of grace.

55

Grace in Accidental Relocation

This story is second-hand. I heard it from my pastoral colleague, Carol Solovitz, but it deserves re-telling. It's a true story about grace from her family home in Kentucky. They were a Church of God family, with strict faith boundaries and even stricter morals, i.e., rules about behavior handed-down from God. Apparently, Carol's great-grandfather had died who, because of his bootlegging and use of moonshine, and was designated for burial outside the church's fenced-in cemetery. Certainly, no one of that incorrigible standing deserved to be buried among the righteous children of God. Maybe God had not so declared, but the brethren of this congregation resolved that God would want it that way. And so, the funeral and burial took place. Almost full - stop! A number of years later, the amount of space for burying the righteous had been used up. "We simply have to expand the cemetery," said the head deacon at a council meeting. "There is a row of trees on the west side of the cemetery, a creek on the north side, and piles of rocks/boulders on the east. The only direction we can possibly expand is to the south." Now, on the south side, the great-grandpa (remember the lover of moonshine?) was buried. Clearly, the only thing worse than originally burying Emil within the cemetery would be to move his grave. God forbid that. Let him rest in peace; he surely had none of God's peace in this life. You can perhaps see where this is going. . . Yep, the fence had to be moved about twenty feet south. Would God approve under such circumstances that great-grandpa would now – by default - be included in the cemetery? The congregation unanimously decided God would. Remember the congregation's (that means God's) hands were tied; what else could they do? Grace for me, is in the final place of great-grandpa's remains (among the faithful), not his earlier plot based on the church council's resolve. Grace is also experienced in my laughter whenever I think of this story. Thanks, Carol.

<h1 style="text-align:center">56</h1>

<h2 style="text-align:center">Grace in a Bobblehead</h2>

It was in response to a note I had sent him about an upcoming lecture in 2009 that (retired) Archbishop Harry Flynn of the Minneapolis St. Paul archdiocese responded with an invitation that I come to his home for lunch. I thought, "Wow, lunch with an archbishop!" And lunch we did, at Harry's beautiful retirement house in the country, northeast of Northfield, Minnesota. A wealthy person gave the archdiocese the house and acres for each retired bishop to use. (I guess they only need one such dwelling since archbishops usually retire at an advanced age.) Harry greeted me that April day, along with his Golden Retriever, and he proceeded to show me his home, including the makeshift chapel off the kitchen that he used each day for his devotions. Harry loved to cook and entertain; the meals he prepared were wonderful, including his homemade soup and dessert. I can vividly remember the aroma in his home that day, like it was yesterday. It was a wonderful lunch hour, the first of several as our friendship grew. A couple of years after this initial occasion at his country home, I invited Harry to preach at Grace Lutheran Church for our Reformation Day services. Now keep in mind that the Reformation is the title for the 16th century breakaway of the 'Lutherans/Protestants' from the Catholics, a breakaway with violent repercussions leading to four centuries of conflict. Of course, volumes of meetings (dialogues) and numerous statements have led to much greater respect and reconciliation, especially since the 1960s and the Second Vatican

Council. Harry knew all this, but/and he graciously accepted our invitation, much like I accepted his invitation for lunch. Harry had a deep commitment to ecumenical relations and building bridges among faith communities. He was known for his gentle manner and reconciling presence. Fast forward to late October and Reformation Sunday that year at Grace Lutheran Church. We rolled-out the red carpet (to compliment his hat and robe) and made a big day of a really big day. The archbishop's sermon was well-crafted and truly appropriate for this historic and ecumenical day in the life of our congregation. At the end of his sermon, I invited the congregation to stand and applaud, which they did with great gusto. I then proceeded to the chancel, shaking Harry's hand and giving him a hug (which is pretty 'intimate' for Lutherans). I handed him a small box with a gift from the congregation, which I encouraged him to open. Inside the box was a Bobblehead of Martin Luther. I said to Harry, "After about 450 years, I think it's time we give Martin Luther back to you, the Roman Catholic Church from which brother Martin came!" He, of course, kindly accepted the gesture and the attempt at humor. History was made on that Reformation Sunday at Grace Lutheran Church of Apple Valley. The historic division – Catholic and Protestant – was acknowledged and 'overruled.' Well, at least in a small way. Archbishop Flynn's Gospel-centered message was truly in the spirit of Jesus, clearly in the spirit of Martin Luther (the catholic turned protester), and beautifully in the spirit of things ecumenical/interfaith as we've entered the Twenty-first century. How grace-filled have these encounters been. Ironic and sacred was our Reformation Day worship on that Sunday.

57

Grace in a Host of Family and Friends

Although there are not enough pages here to detail the complexion of all my grace-filled family and friendships, I do want to list by name some of those people, not included above, who, over a lifetime, have provided me with daily/weekly doses of grace. These relationships are ironic because they show 'Grace in the Ordinary.' There's always a risk of omitting someone who belongs on that list, but naming these important people overrides my fear of omitting some. I'm talking about Karen and Sharon, Gary and Lee, Ron and Becky, Faye and Shirley, Marty and Lon, Kip and Deb, Dick and Judy and Dan and Jill, Vince and Arnold and Dave and Elisabeth, Charlie and Carol, Janet, Cliff and Laurel, Elise and Tybo, Ron and Luis and Barry and Paul, Bonita and Jerry and Marilyn and Jerry, David and Gloria, Elise and Thad, Jeff and Marcia, Bonnie, Joel and John and Jenny and Gaylon and Gottfried, Michael and Keith, Pat and John and Nancy, Larry and Dee, Mark and Laurie, Stephen and Andras, Bruce and Verna, Kim and Di, Dan and Chris; my God-children, Kristin and Kirsten, Ben and Brian; my extended family - my in-laws - includes: Darrell and Gail; Kristen, Melissa and Amanda, Cheryl and Chad and Ryland, Lisa and Dimitri and Olivia and Nathan; Becky and David, Jen and Tony and Morgan and Madison, Jason and Lee and Emma; James; Jeff and Lisa, Luke and Jessica and Blake and Lyla and Josie. Grace comes in so many shapes and so many sizes. For these ordinary friends and wonderful family, I have been graciously blessed.

Inconclusive Statement of Faith

I am a Christian by baptism, confirmation, ordination and community. Jesus is the primary window through which I have come to experience the ultimate grace of God and one of the faces - perhaps the first - I expect to meet at the Heavenly Gate. I, a Christian in almost every way, am eternally grateful for Jesus, St. Paul, et.al., who understood the grace-filled Covenant of Israel to include even us lost Gentiles. Consistent with Jewish belief that God created and is present in every square inch of creation through Yahweh's rua'ch (Spirit), and as evidenced in Jesus' loving embrace of the people he met, and reflective of Islam's conviction that Allah's goodness is ever-present and incredibly grace-filled, I have been blessed to learn of the ever - greater and expansive grace of God - 50+ shapes - in almost every square inch of creation that I have visited. And so, as much as I will be forever grateful for the Jesus who talked with the Samaritan Woman, accepted Nicodemus' invitation for a drink, healed any number of hurting bodies and souls, and said from Golgotha's Hill, "Father, forgive them, for they know not what they do," I will also be temporally grateful for the shapes of grace that have visited me in the most common, unlikely people, places, and events one could imagine. A significant dimension of the Lutheran-Christian faith that I inherited emphasizes the 'moral imperative.' That is, faith in Jesus Christ is not merely the acceptance of God's redeeming love and gracious embrace; implicit in the salvation we have received is the imperative to share what we have received, that same love and embrace every place we go, with every person we meet, during every day of our lives. Salvation is not a gift to be hoarded but rather a shared relationship. For me, this moral imperative involves not only activities and events, but, equally important, a way of speaking with others. St. Paul's words to the congregation at Ephesus beautifully encourage such a way of speaking: "Let no evil talk come out of your mouths, but only what is useful for building up, as there is need, so that your words may impart grace to those who hear." That verse is my prayer. I expect I will have much more grace to experience. At least until the day and hour that I meet the eternal God of grace, face to face. Just as I continue to experience day after day more shapes of grace and express that in words and deeds akin to Jesus, I hope that you - the reader - will also discover shapes of grace that far exceed fifty